The Becoming Years

18 to 28

G. A. Wray

Adventures In Thought

The Becoming Years

living your life between ages

18 to 28

Is first about ending your
lifelong dependent state from infant to18 years
and achieving your own Self Direction

Creating a career is secondary

A human life is in major development

The Ten years It Takes
To get over being a Kid

The Thoughts you need
to Make Sure It Happens

Before 18 are your **Growing up Years**

18 to 28 are your **Becoming Years**

To enable the rest of your life

The Becoming Years

G. A. Wray, author of this book, may be contacted by email at author@thebecomingyears.com.

For school classes, multiple copies may also be purchased from the Internet website thebecomingyears.com.

Cataloging-in-Publication Data on file with the Library of Congress. Printed in the United States of America

ISBN 978-0-9903721-0-3   First Edition

Art work on cover by Steven Power
www.powergalleryhawaii.com

Acknowledging with special appreciation for -

Cover design by Emily Matheny
Print production direction by Krissy Roper
Editing review by Bruce Willis

Special Thanks for the many student critiques, particularly for the keen perceptions of Ian Akers and Toby Perelmuter - 2014 high school graduates.

Contents

Title page

Quotations Remembered…...…..................…...........xi

A Prologue - Born and Beautiful…....................,,,,xiii

CHAPTERS

1. **Remembering 18 -**
   The Beginning of Becoming............................…...1

2. **What you know about everyone**
   you have never met.....................................…....7

3. **You are a Song - that only you can sing**
   Appreciating yourself – being unique 17

4. **Self Possession -**
   Hanging onto your uniqueness......................22

5. What people really want from you –
   A cross cultural constant.................................27

6. Intelligent People - Who are They?
   How do you know if the people you meet
   are reliably smart?..47

7. The Clear Grasp of Youth –
   You Do Not Want to Lose
   The directness of Individual perception..........55

8. Who are You?
   You are not the horse you ride.........................67

9. A Keyhole to Understanding Personality
   Look for the organizing power of fear.............73

10. Self Esteem - A Reality Twisted......................85

11. When Will You Know that You Have
    Grown-up? A Test............................93

12. Managing Your Mind -
    the Freedom of Self Direction - Knowing
    how to think the thoughts you want............107

13. The Engineering of Luck...............................117

14. Encountering Genetics
    Be aware - Go easy..127

15. Confronting the Rocks of Genetics -
    In Personalities...135

16. On Loving What You Are Born With -
    But what if you don't.....................................139

17. Joining the Traffic of Impersonal Humanity -
    Leaving the Road of Growing-up................149

18. **The Pixel People in your Life**
    Taking the shine off your humanity.............155

19. **Details are Fuel for Glory**
    In the engine room of decisions -
    your new attitude...167

20. **Managing What People Expect from You**
    Creating the one reputation
    you really want..175

21. **Is it in your Nature to be a Professional?**
    Do you want to be
    a person who is trusted?...............................191

22. **Government - Corking a Violent Volcano**
    Your private thoughts about government...199

23. **Resolving Conflicts - Looking to the Future**
    How to think about Courts
    and Lawyers..221

24. Showing You are not a Simple Mind
A scientific proof..233

25. Managing Your Internet Exposure
A 21st century essential.................................243

26. How Do You Know - Who You Can Trust?
Fundamentals of trusting people
recently met...257

27. Really Smart Young People
Really Need a Mentor -
How do you find yours?..................................269

28. Discovering Your Attitude
What other people can see in you.................277

29. Why It Takes Ten Years
to Get Over a Being a Kid..............................285

30. **The Roads We All Take -
The Paths Underfoot
Do we know why?**..297

An Epilogue - 307

An Author's Note - ………………………..….309

It is easier to build strong youths than to repair broken men

Frederick Douglass 1895

The basic ideas first realized
on beginning adulthood
are the trees that proudly line the road
for the rest of life

A PROLOGUE

BORN AND BEAUTIFUL

Well, here you are. Born and beautiful. And wondering through your years of 18 to 28.

Everyone does it. So what is special? Actually, two things, and they are once-in-a life-time special: the never before experienced difficulties to be encountered in a new-to-you impersonal world, and the never ending consequences of not taking charge of yourself between 18 and 28, and making yourself go from a kid's world of dependent direction to the really free world of self direction.

You will easily see this - as we go thru all the everyday unknowing that will confront you.

How you handle these ten years between 18 and 28 will solidly shape your forthcoming life - your existence.

The Becoming Years

There will be no other time of your living where your sensibilities will be so totally confronted, and even assaulted with new life situations to manage - because at about 18, you're just finished with your needing to be a kid.

The need to master all this fresh confrontation that happens only between 18 to 28 years of age, is what makes these ten years more important to you than any other ten years in your life.

You will see how it fully takes these ten years for you to get over your living limitations as a child - or a big kid. It is a huge change. Your chief experience in living as a kid growing up, has been your understanding that you could not survive on your own. And your whole world was a prison type dependency on others, under a prison guard type control by people bigger, stronger than you. These are the crude facts of your growing up years.

This position in life is all you have ever known in your first eighteen years, since you woke up on this planet. And now after 18, you have to replace that imposed lifestyle with one of your own making.

And you have never done this before.

But first let's look at the child life style. It is a capsule - out of which you have to wiggle. And wiggle means you have to struggle. It is not a clean operation. And it certainly is not simple and easy.

Getting over being a child means being your own person, with calm and confidence. It means coming to a poise, where you are self directed, and can decide on things without reference to any tying dependence on your parents - or other people.

It means you must now decide how your parents will fit into your ongoing life as a close companion adult, not as a close controlling adult.

Don't just expect them to understand, which is what you did as a kid. It will be hard for them to treat you differently as an adult. It means guiding your parents, giving your own leadership to their new relationship with you in every day life.

From your beginning, your parents defined your relationship to them. But when you are no longer a growing-up little person, you must firmly take the initiative, and see to it that this relationship is on a path to reflect your new reality.

This is hard, really hard for everyone. You will have to summon all the strength of your character to pull it off. As time goes on now, you have to do a U turn in your mind, where you go back over all the things you are accustomed to doing, but this time as you drive along, you eliminate all the scenery of parents controlling.

And you practice doing it, until it becomes second nature for your life to belong just to yourself, and you become a self-directing creature of your free will. You come to own yourself as a human being. Not easy. You can say it in ten seconds, but it will fully take ten years to reconfigure the child context and content in your mind and its reactions.

This is entering a new landscape. This journey takes fully ten years for almost everyone, though you should have done what you can do by age 26, with two years left to make yourself steady in place.

Ten years to stop and go in taking the chains off, link by link. No matter how you try, this is not going to happen overnight. There are just too many connections, too much to unwind. But if you have not been able to go from parental direction to a basic self direction by age 28, you probably never will.

Sadly, some people never finish the job, and remain partial children all their lives. You are not to let that happen to you.

About 18 years of age, the all encompassing personal family relationships get gradually forced to the back of your consciousness in daily living. The things you must do after 18, working a job or attending a college, abruptly require you to deal with people you have never met, and who don't belong to your family world. You cannot think of two things at once. So you are going to be spending more time thinking about new people you have to deal with. Less time will be available for the family relations that surrounded you in growing up.

After 18 you are entering the impersonal world. Big change. Breathtaking. You are thrown among people, who are not your mother or father - and definitely do not want to be your father or mother. A rude experience. Your normal everyday expectations to have people show concern for you, can be just blown away.

You are basically left to work through this on your own. For everyone at this stage, this can be a seriously unpleasant experience, full of uncertainty and apprehension.

The Chapters that follow now, are a collection of rocks and mountain tops that you will have to stumble across on your way to becoming 28 and by that time, a self directed personality.

Each of the Chapters covers what is likely to be a new way of focusing or thinking about issues you will confront. Most importantly, each Chapter is about a new reaching out, an exercise in using self direction, and taking control in a particular but common circumstance.

You will want to experience the thoughts that will free you from all the beginning gear of growing up - meaning whatever you used as toys and tricycles that were part of your tumbling thinking in day to day life as a kid. You are now free to possess the clearness of mind to become yourself - meaning the delight of your self that comes from your own direction.

So instead of waiting until you suddenly encounter the urgent need to have some resolving ideas about issues that will abruptly confront you, let's set them out now. We can predict most.

You will want your own thought-out answers. To do this, you first need the thought-out questions that will cover your range of needs for a life that you want to be self directed, not parent directed, or other people directed.

Anticipating them now, working thru them now, getting a grasp, and acquiring now a knowledgeable approach and attitude, will keep you sailing smoothly ahead with a solid confidence.

Then you, more than others, will have greater, quicker, insight about what's going on around you.

And you will come to have the good judgment that results from heightened awareness of advance thinking on the basics of everyday encounters on the road beyond 18. It's worth the effort.

Such advanced discernment among the young is rare. So be rare.

An advance note on the chapters ahead:

The writing here is intent on enabling and ensuring an understanding. So there will be themes often repeated from different standpoints. /gw

Chapter 1

REMEMBERING 18 - the Beginning of Becoming

Remember the moment turning 18 years old? If you had any sense you would know you were soon to leave the jailed scene of being totally controlled by parents, and of being legally untrusted by society as a minor.

Freedom, at last you think. But never having lived a free life, you couldn't possibly know what it really is, and what it really means long term.

So being eighteen and somewhat free at last, what's next? You're headed to a new world of relating to people. Before 18, everything is personal, very personal in your relations with your fellow human beings. Now at eighteen years of age, this totally personal way of living will fade.

No one has probably sat you down, and clearly told you that after you hit 18 years, you are going to start to enter and meander thru a forest of human beings who have absolutely no interest in being your mother or father, friend or relative. Your are going to encounter people who will shock you in being different from what you are used to in daily life - primarily by being indifferent, just indifferent to you. It's not comfortable.

Did any of the adults around you at the time, take you aside, and warn you about entering an impersonal world? For most young people, the answer is just "no."

No one bothered to mention it. Presumably, this is explained by the fact that they had to go thru this themselves without any help; so why bother. Everybody is hit with this, so you'll be all right in the end. Possibly so.

But going forward, with some understanding in advance, will take a lot of the unhappiness out of being young - that comes with uncertainty about your personal future. It will let you cut some of the misery from not being able to see clearly what's going on around you in the impersonal world, and ahead.

So beyond 18, somewhat abruptly, you will increasingly meet and deal with people who do not really care about you. You will be free. But you will be walking around this planet, an impersonal world, with people who can be as cold and impersonal as the stars that surround it.

And you need to pay attention and confront the difference between the personal world in which you were confined in growing up, and the new expansive void of disinterest about you in which you are about to be immersed.

It can be bewildering and ugly. At some point you will just pause and ask yourself: what's a nice person like me doing on this planet?

You can no longer be a happy puppy waking up in the morning, not worried about the people that will happen to you - that will cross your path during your day. You have yet to experience that within this impersonal world of human beings, you will find people who can be worse than you could ever have known.

Beyond 18, as the terrain gets more unknown and tougher, you also get increasing problems in figuring out what direction you want to take, and why. You will be having problems figuring out exactly what you want to do; well, actually, what you really want.

What you really want? This is the annoying unspoken question that now accompanies and complicates your new confrontation with impersonal humans after becoming 18.

It is then that you have to seriously ask yourself: What am I supposed to do, really? How do I know what I want? Is it just a career, I am supposed to worry about?

Uncertainty about this, uncertainty about yourself, uncertainty about new people, and you have opportunities for confusion never before experienced.

Tough times are ahead. Let's talk about them now, and get at least some guiding attitudes on confronting people that you will have to manage, like the difficult personalities you will have to deal with, the dopey educated, even the forceful government and it's bureaucrats, your immediate boss on the job, and fellow workers you will be assembled with.

Then- there are those other people you will be meeting along the way who will look at you, and put you off with their brief curious interest in you - like a fish looking you over.

You want to pause and gather mind centering attitudes towards government power, the play of law courts, the urban myths of science sponsored advice, and the false certainty of its speculation, the substance of making decisions, organizing your impact in meetings. You need to be clear about the one personal reputation you have to foster in dealing with an impersonal world. You will want to keep about yourself the companions of clarity and courage to make judgments.

You need to learn to manage and love your own mind and trust your intuition. You need to be self aware of the impact of media absorbing you - cumulatively dulling the awareness of your own self being alive and dulling your dealing with all that surrounds you.

You will want to thrive on your own unique and intuitive glances at the world - that comes with being free of excessive media input. You will need to have your own rules to control this intrusive force.

The Internet is huge in your life. Your need to be actively street smart in its use, is equally huge.

It is better to have some thought-out attitudes for managing all this.

This can be the moment to do this - here and now.

Before your 18th birthday, the world was something that was just happening to you.

After 18, you become something that is happening to the world.

Chapter 2

WHAT YOU KNOW ABOUT EVERYONE YOU HAVE NEVER MET

Your childhood is gone. You have a world full of people before you. People you have yet to meet.

So ask yourself this curious question: What can I know about people I have never met?

Picture yourself about to walk up to a person. You are about to be introduced. As you approach, should your mind be blank, ready to deal with whatever is said and offered to you?

No. You are going to approach this new person, poised, and keenly aware of some very personal things about this human being you know quite well.

So what can you personally know about a person you have never met, or even heard about?

You think the quick honest answer is nothing? Really ?

Wrong. You do know - a lot - some important very personal stuff - of which you both are acutely aware.

Look at yourself. Not too long ago, you were born. You first saw light. You were then introduced to a nice person, who said she was your mother. Then there should have been someone right after that, who said he was your father.

You had nothing to do with choosing these people. It was done for you.

You had nothing to do with choosing the place on this planet where all this happened; but you are stuck with the locale of where it did.

You did not choose it.

The time, the year, the month, the day when you began, was imposed on you.

So here you are, living with people you didn't choose, and you have been put in a place on this planet that you also did not choose. No consultation about the timing.

Worse. You were given a body off the rack. No chance to choose skin color, curly hair or not, tall or short? No choice. Sex? What you see is what you got. No consultation. None.

How fair is this! Everyone is equally treated this abruptly, and then bulldozed over the edge of nothingness into life.

What can you say? Well say truthfully what you do know: that we all wake up to the reality of living in the same boat - called "Zero Choice".

Anyone of us could have had, what befell to some other person. Think about it. The entire body platform and social platform on which your person begins to exist, is something upon which you were plopped - just dropped. So for what you got, you cannot be blamed. Nor can you be praised for what you were born with, as your own achievement.

This is the first fact of life to be learned about ourselves, and to be understood about other people as we meet them for the first time. They have had the exact same unruly experience of being thrust into a body and into unchosen conditions of living, as you have experienced.

We know this about each other when meeting for the first time, and mutually glancing at our faces and bodies.

So we do not blame ourselves for our condition. For the same reason, we cannot blame other people for theirs.

This means we approach each other, especially the people we don't know, with this pre-knowledge and awareness: that we have in common this same confrontation of dealing with the brute force experience of coming to life with conditions imposed.

This is what we very personally know about every person we have not met.

We should approach each other with this awareness, because it is truth.   In this awareness, we owe each other an immediate empathy of understanding when we see physical characteristics that are usually quick to be derided, like being really short in height, or having a large nose, or weird looking eyes and ears, anything not ordinary. We cannot demean each other for this.

On meeting for the first time, we have to control our reaction with empathy - a sympathetic understanding of each other's imposed reality, a very mutual reality.

Think about this. We have no choice as to how we are going to look and appear to other people. Nor they to us. So when we meet an odd appearing person, not pleasant to look at, we get real. We back off any demeaning dismissal. We understand that the "chance of life" has awarded this individual a difficulty.

And when you see a person's family condition or social status, you will know this did not arise or begin out of personal choice. It is forced on everyone as to who they begin living with, and where on the planet in the beginning of life, they will be growing up.

So let's give reality a break - and understand this. Every one you will ever meet has had this same no-choice tumble-into-life experience.

No discussion, no questions, and Boom, you are suddenly someone being somewhere.

Then once the fire of life is lit and burning, we all have to deal with the same choices. Though surrounded by people, we are left to ponder: who else is going to know us? Whom are we going to know? Here we have at least some choice as to when and how (in what manner).

Reflect slowly on all this - because what has happened so rudely to you - no choices allowed - has also happened in the same personal, intimate, abrupt way to every single individual you will ever meet.

Being so arbitrarily brought to life is something people just don't talk to each other about.

Nor do they talk about their mutual awareness that each of us lives in this same hollowed empty cavern looking and waiting for answers: how come this happened to me, and what's next? and Why?

This haunting wait for answers, and seeking the 'why' of life, is also a mutual consciousness you have with each human individual you will ever encounter.

If you carry this level of awareness as an empathetic mindset when you meet new people, your approach will be one of a willing acceptance of differences, no matter how dramatic they may be. Your initial uncritical stance before them will be sensed, and seen as your direct and personal interest in them, replacing and warding off any hostility or anxiety of acceptance.

This certainty of something to be mutually understood, is a "joining" approach to meeting new people. People easily sense when a person meeting them has a stance of sharing a mutual empathy, and they react naturally with relaxed interest - being less wary.

Because you make yourself conscious of everyone's beginning personal truth, you can bring to the moment of meeting a calmness and directness that invites an honest mutual awareness. As a consequence, some observers will think your ability to relate to people is charismatic. Something hard to define. Your awareness would be the reason. So let it happen.

Try to separate the person from the body you see. And speak to the person, not to their physical appearance.

Hard to do? Yes. But you do it because you possess this discernment of basic truth. And you show it in your demeanor. And it is called 'class'.

One day you will pass by a dock. You will see some wretched looking worker bent over loading cargo. He looks like he is from a dark and distant country. How could you, glancing at him, have the slightest knowledge of what goes on in his unspoken consciousness. But you do. He was assaulted with the same sudden circumstances of an unchosen birth, as you were. He has the same nuclear fire in his belly that uniquely says "I am", as you do. Physically, you could not appear to be more different. Yet on a personal level, you have much in common.

Each of you were just shoved into the same river of conscious existence, plunging over the same waterfalls of time.

If communication could occur on this level, there would be a very mutual understanding. No conscious human being is beyond the draw of an offer of this understanding personal approach from another human person, such as yourself.

Meeting strangers, however briefly, and wordlessly contemplating them with this primal understanding, has intuitive consequences. It creates an initial perception of empathy; induces a natural engagement; and invites in a blink, a natural willingness to like each other.

Sooner or later, everyone picks up a standard way of pleasantly meeting new people. There is a passing show of pretended interest. No serious thinking.

But you can be different. You can meet a new person with a deliberate pause (however slight) upon just meeting. A moment to engage your awareness that you are now meeting a human being just as puzzled as you are to be alive. This is the pause that connects - without a word. it gives space for a mutual understanding to engage.

The pause is a poise that can speak volumes.

All we really have on this planet are each other.

Pleasantly meeting new people,with a good natured "hello and goodbye" is usually taken to mean nothing. But you are young, and you are allowed to be different. And you can pause to be personally genuine in an instant meeting, where this is not normally done by older people, numbed by the routine of living.

Worth a try - because It is hard not to comment and observe that:

It is astonishing what can happen in an instant of mutual understanding - between two people freshly meeting.

It was a mere song in an old musical play (Hello Dolly) that evoked in a simple lyric the ultimate in our seeking: "It only takes a moment to be loved a whole life long."

Chapter 3

You Are a Song - That Only You Can Sing

Appreciating yourself - on being unique

So much of growing up has been with the ever present worry of what people think of you. And why not?

You are new to this game of life. You have spent so much time being smaller than the people around you, and really needing their help and approval to survive.

But stop a moment. Try to look at yourself - just yourself- looking at yourself.

Give yourself a moment of situational awareness. Just you - alone - looking at everything you see around you; and just you - alone - thinking of all that you know.   What strikes you?

Well, it is very cool. You will see at once that there is only one of you.

You are a singularity on this planet, and you know it.

You are in fact, unique. You know with certainty that there has never been another "you" - anywhere or ever. When you say "I exist", the world and all that exists, or ever has existed, has never heard this before, and never will except from you.

So when you do anything, anything at all, the world has never before seen it done-- by you.

When you first say to another person, "I love you", the world has never heard this before. Because it has never heard you saying it. And when you decline to say it, the world can never find a substitute. Because there is no substitute for you.

If the world should lose you, you can never be replaced. It is just the way it is.

The importance of you being you, can never be exaggerated. You are a happening - to all of existence. And the world has never experienced you before.

So what you do, what you choose to do, becomes a unique experience to all of existence.

You are a song that only you can sing.

And whatever you fail to do, will never be the same if done by someone else. What you fail to do will be forever undone, as an act of yourself.

So what you have going, is awesome. Something forever is going to be, or not be - depending on what you decide to do.

Everyone knows something that no one else does.

It begins in knowing what it is to be you. In the entire parade of humanity, there is no one else that will know this.

The mystery of being you, will never be solved, except by yourself on this planet. Nor can you ever be fully known by another human being, because you are a unique happening, that can go in any direction at any second, on the instance of your will.

Your awareness of your own uniqueness is the poise of your self possession. It is the pedestal on which you should stand, and direct the force and energy of your life.

You should understand that the uniqueness of your existence is also an unchangeable reality that can never be taken from you.

The uniqueness of your living underlies the solid confident appreciation you must have of yourself - just in existing.

You only become a full force human being when you direct your energy of living with a consciousness of the unique nature of your every effort to touch the world around you.

It gives you the satisfaction and confidence that there is a potential meaning of incalculable importance to what you choose to do, and whom you will choose to love.

No one, nor any circumstance, can take away or diminish the unique character of who you are. You need not remind people of your uniqueness. But you should carry an unspoken attitude that reflects your own solid understanding of the personal uniqueness of your life. This personal confidence will, in turn, have an effect on how people relate to you.

It will, in an unspoken way, create respect for you that reflects your own attitude towards yourself as a unique person. The resulting confidence in yourself, is something that people will readily perceive, and more often than not, respond to with spontaneous respect.

As long as you understand this, then the observations, opinions and criticisms of other people, are not critical to the stature of your life, nor can they undermine your basic confidence.

Bottom line:

No matter what happens, you stand tall, directing the energy of your unique existence, giving life to the truth you know.

Welcome yourself to the beauty of being - being your unique self.

The world awaits your self expression.

Chapter 4

SELF POSSESSION

Hanging on to Your Uniqueness

Self possession. A strange word. Why say it? Because It means something important you have not done.

You have not given control of your own person - yourself - to other people on this planet. This is hard to avoid.

Everyone, by the nature of being a person, wants approval - wants to be desired by other persons. It is a built-in yearning from birth.

Wanting this approval is one thing. But if you let wanting it, turn into your requiring it, then this is quite another story. That is how you lose yourself - lose your self possession.

A life of demanding from others an approval of yourself, is a personal destruction, a kind of self inflicted personal suicide. It is a fool's insistence. Because you are making yourself a conditional reality, dependent on other people choosing to approve your self, or not.

This becomes a denial of your own personal being, a discarding of your own uniqueness that exists precisely because your being belongs to no other human person's will, but your own. And you give this away when you make a condition of your life that other human persons must approve and desire your existence.

The self-uniqueness of your existence is not subject to the approval of your fellow human beings, unless you would so choose - and thoughtlessly - or by habit - allow it to happen.

Nevertheless, you have this built-in yearning that says you are not complete until you have your existence asserted and wanted and approved by other persons. This is a yearning that will last a lifetime, and will never be fulfilled or satisfied. You will never know anyone that has achieved this. There is a reason for this. You may come to know it.

But meanwhile, understand this: no one can compete with you being you. You are beyond the possibility of competition. You stand free. Unassailable as you are - now. No one can diminish the uniqueness of your existence. You are rock solid as yourself, alive and unique.

When you get this settled view of yourself, that your self at it's core cannot be threatened, then your mind and all it's powers will be more free to perform.

You can relax in the core of your own being. The uniqueness of being yourself, is indestructible.

When a human being says quietly to himself: " I exist", is there any possibility of confusing him with another human being who says the same thing?

The conscious "I" is singular. Some thing is absolutely unique or not, depending on whether it can ever be replicated. Identical twins can be born a perfect match. But the person that says "I", "I will", or "I won't " is totally separate.

So take a cosmic view of yourself. You don't know, nor do any of us have a clear idea of what we will become after we leave this planet. But we do know that while we are here, in the halls of time, each of us, one by one, are unique to the world's experience, and to all of it's history.

And what you can give to the world is your affirmation of what you understand. This is something no one has ever experienced before - your understanding - because it is you being unique, asserting your awareness.

You got to love the possibilities - of you being you. Standing tall, confronting all that is. And what you can uniquely do, and mean to others.

So what do you do with these thoughts? This self awareness? You make it the core of an indestructible calmness and confidence. You are the 100 percent owner of the being that you are - no matter what happens to you.

So what does all this amount to? Getting yourself a clear sense of indestructibility as a unique being, and, bereft of fear, you are free to stand tall in the world around you,

By your nature of being, you will be seeking the approval - the desire - (the love) of other persons, which you cannot command. What you are seeking is the desiring of your existence, but only by the free will of another person. And that free will that you wish to support you, can, by being a free will, also freely decline.

But you know that nothing can ever diminish the self that is uniquely yours.

.

Having a strong sense of self is a poise that is pleasing to people around you. You will see that humans are attracted to those among them that have this strong confident sense of self. With it comes a general certainty and calmness of manner. They see a face lacking fear.

People see strength in such a person. A clear sense of self. But to be such a person, you need to choose to think the thoughts about yourself that understands and celebrates that reality of being the only you in existence - your personal uniqueness.

So let nothing distract your determination to affirm your self as a person absolutely unique to your world - never compromising yourself by a need to be desired. This is self possession.

What the world needs from you, is this self assertion.

Chapter 5

WHAT PEOPLE REALLY WANT FROM YOU

A CROSS CULTURAL CONSTANT

Do people you don't know, want something from you?   Personally?

Yes, they do, and they want it non-stop.

Diving into the impersonal world as you must - into this endless sea of people you do not know - you should be clearly forewarned if there is anything these unknown people may, in fact, actually want from you.

You should be clearly aware if there is any kind of desire involving you that everyone of them - all of them - would have. If there is such a thing, then there is a huge understanding here, that awaits your keen awareness.

And there is such a thing. It exists. It is never discussed. Yet this desire involving you is a cross cultural constant in every human being, in every human civilization.

It is easy to declare what it is. It is so simple, it is initially hard to grasp.

It is this: everyone's all embracing drive to have one's personal being desired by other human persons.

This is a "won't go away" desire that is built into the machinery of every individual person, one by one. No exceptions. It is there from the moment of each person's birth. It is so all-the-time present in everyone at every instant, that people fail to single this out and define it.

Sounds simple. It actually is not. This desire, this yearning is in the nature of being a person, and is an uncomplicated expression built into human consciousness. What is complicated, is obtaining the satisfaction of this desire from other human persons when you enter their arena of awareness.

They can choose not to respond. All persons have a free will.

You can reflect that you will never meet or know of a human who has fully satisfied this life yearning. People move from one place to another, from one house to a different one with a fresh view, and a new landscape of scenery and relationships, expecting fresh possibilities of exciting life satisfaction. But in the end, it is always about people. It always falls short. And you are off to a new place. But it is not about searching for a new place. It is about searching for new people.

Beautiful places need beautiful people - to keep you there. Beautiful people meaning having people with you that will satisfy that yearning for close relationships desiring you.

But if such are not with you, you remain faced with that ever present and unsettling and unsatisfied requirement of this human yearning for finding people approving and wanting you to be. A lack of this fulfillment will eventually drive you after awhile to keep moving - when and if you can.

So this yearning to be desired by other persons, is constantly underfoot. You don't buy an amazing car to impress your dog. Apart from your own delight in design, color, and performance, it is most often other people's approval that is the reason for your effort to have an impressive expensive looking car, as well as nice clothes with popular brands, and great haircuts.

To put it simply, you want to be looked upon, and approved by other people. To put it technically, you are acting to have your own personal existence to be desired and so to be asserted by other persons.

In sum, everyone has this primal born-with yearning to want their individual personal existence recognized, asserted and approved. In a single word, they want their existence to be 'desired' by other individual people around them. The word "loved" would be more accurately used here, but it carries the loose baggage of an easy "come and go" meaning.

This drive to have one's personal being desired by other human persons is an all embracing environment - like the air everyone breathes. Ultimately, this is what everyone wants from you - your desiring them. The essence of living is this personal drive. And this 'desiring' is the dynamic - guiding force of its energy.

This means it is present in every human person regardless of culture, ethnicity, or race. In recorded history, its presence has been continually affirmed.

It has never altered. It is a powerful engine you are born with, and it comes turned on from day one.

Indeed, if you were to ever ask in an abstract moment: Do you really have to care about other people liking you? The answer is yes - constantly - absolutely. But why?

The reason can be philosophically discerned. But that effort is not for this moment. The concern to be dealt with here and now is that it exists. It is a central dynamic of every person you will ever meet or know about. It is the power source driving their history of striving, during their lifetime - whatever it turns out to be - from loving to fighting, or conquering or giving.

Until you accept an understanding of this universal and primal personal desire of every human individual to have one's own existence expressed as wanted, approved and desired by other human persons, you will be one of those human beings who just never "gets" the gist of other people.

This desire lives at the root of awareness in everyone. And It doesn't take much to bring it immediately to the surface in a conscious focus. And when it does surface, the energy behind it comes with an almost instinctive ferocity.

It can be startling. You suddenly know a deep desire, a primal nerve, has been touched.

All of this calls for a way of thinking about each other that is so fundamental that its recognition is not part of everyday expression. It remains mostly buried. But in the daily on-going experience with each other, it can at times suddenly and clearly emerge.

A case in point. While teaching an ethics course in a university MBA program, the issue came up in class discussion about responding to verbal attacks. An odd but interesting question was raised as to what is the worst thing that could ever be said to anyone. The responses were all over the map, ending in crude, offensive, horrendous language. The class became uneasy. They haltingly ran out of words and ideas trying to capture the worst that could be said to a fellow human being.

Think about it. Conjuring the worst words you can say to another person is not a simple task. It is a real test of one's imagination. The possibilities seem to have no end. But you have to know where to look.

Finally, I told them I would give them a very different response as to what would be the very worst, the most offensive thing, you could ever say to anyone.

I told them It would be just four words. Each word would not be offensive, but together, once said to anyone, they would be explosive, and would never be forgotten.

It is to look directly at some human person, and say quietly: "You should not exist."

And when I slowly and deliberately said this, I saw a girl, near the front of the class, shudder slightly. The 24 students in the class seem to freeze for a moment, sounds stopped. There was an instant second of shock. A visceral reaction.

For a long almost half minute the room was still. It just seemed to shut everyone down. No one offered a comment except one girl who asked: "Then, what is the best thing you can say to a person?"

There was only one possible response. I hesitated to say it, as we were going way beyond the subject matter of the course. But I started this, and knew it should be answered.

What is the best thing you can say to another human being? It surely is this:

"If I were God, I would have created you with all my heart."

There was silence - again. I had created a private moment for everyone. Nothing was said. But after class, a student passed by, and said quickly to me as he turned to go: "that best thing, was the best I have ever heard." He walked off.

It was simply said.   But this tells us that there is a truth here,   that is seldom spoken out loud: This wanting one's personal existence, one's sheer being, to be really desired by another person, is the fuel for the nuclear fire of yearning at the core of everyone's consciousness.

When you comprehend another person is expressing freely to you "I want you to be", this targets your most intimate sense of being alive. For it is a human's ultimate fulfillment when another person effectively says to him: I am glad you exist. I want you to be.

But how could this be true, if we never talk to each other in these terms?

The answer is, however, that indeed we do deal with each other in very clear terms of wanting our existence to be desired by our fellow humans. It is not starkly said. Almost never actually said. But It happens so continually and so naturally, we hardly reflect on it - because it is happening every moment, and our lives are surrounded by its expression.

Begin with getting up in the morning. More goes on than routine body maintenance.

Step in front of the mirror. You already know what you look like. But what happens next are deliberate acts of making yourself pleasing to look at. You don't have your dog in mind. It is to please other humans that you apply cosmetics, eliminate blemishes and enhance how you will look to other people, all to avoid personal disapproval - meaning you want to be desirable to your fellow humans.

A huge global industry supports this universal human need to be desirable to the people who are alive with us on this planet. You begin with a daily routine of making your personal appearance attractive and pleasing to the people you will meet before going to sleep again. Most people do not like to specifically admit this. But it is factually true.

This unspoken drive supports a cosmetic industry that is constantly developing new and inventive ways for an individual to enhance his or her desirability in every conceivable manner.

The cosmetic industry knows you will buy products that will evoke compliments about yourself, that will single you out for special desirability from the crowds of other people seeking attention and notice from each other.

This "making yourself desirable" driven cosmetic industry has always existed in recorded human history. It exists absolutely in every culture on this planet.

How humanly universal is this "seeking personal desirability" effort of the cosmetic industry?

The hard facts are these: The entire worldwide cosmetic industry sales in the year 2012 reached over $170 Billion dollars. It's distributed fairly uniformly around the world with ~$40 billion in the Americas, ~$60 billion in Europe, ~$60 billion in Australia & Asia, and another $10 billion in Africa.

It is everywhere around this planet. Consider exactly what people are spending their money on. The cosmetic industry (beauty industry) can be broken down into 4 major segments: Hair, Skin, Fragrance, and Makeup.

In history, this is a deeply rooted human activity. Again, rooted in what? Rooted in the innate desire of a human person to have their own personal being, their own existence, to be desired and approved by other persons. Without this desire, peculiar to humans, there would be no cosmetic industry.

The world's birds and animals do not have this everyday desire. Instinctual preening for sex is as far as they go.   With humans there is something else going on. The human desire for approval is part of their every moment of awareness - all day long.

So why don't we cut to the chase, just say it out loud: "I want the existence of me to be endorsed and loved and honored by my fellow humans living with me in my time. I want to see people wanting me."

Why is nobody straight forward about this?

Your probable answer will be just shy of bewilderment. The reason is a mystery and the reason is obvious. It is a mystery because everyone acts the part but say nothing, So how could you know.

You can also observe that the reason is obvious because you can well understand that this candid declaration, would more likely put people off, than attract them. People don't like being confronted with a demand for their personal affections, which is a demand to force their free will. Such demands are the enemy of a free will, and makes us turn away.

So no one says anything. But our day is filled with setting the table, to encourage people to find us attractive, and desirable, and wanting us to be. Making yourself look attractive and desirable is a daily major effort, but no one speaks of the reason.

Weight loss programs are hugely popular for adults. It is big business, advertised everywhere for health reasons, but more explicitly for making you more slim and attractive to be looked at by your fellow humans whose approval you seek.

But no advertisements ever explain the reason why in the first place you would want to be desired by other people. It is just 'sort of' understood. We don't discuss this. No explanation seems to be necessary, as if there is an assumption here that it is well understood. (Perhaps not, because seldom does anyone really think it through.)

Annual expenditures for these weight loss programs are $20 Billion in the United State alone in the year 2012. The motivation for the bulk of this money is clearly for gaining attractiveness and personal approval, rather than from a health motivation, as the content of the industry advertising actually indicates.

Clothing is noted for their well regarded brand names when it has their signature word embroidered in easy to see places. Why is this costly embroidered brand name a reason for buying what is otherwise just a nice piece of clothing? Because when seen by other people, it tells them that you have money to buy expensive clothing which every well known brand name deliberately elevates in retail cost. It preys upon the human person's craving to be desired and approved by their fellow humans in displaying one's self as one who has economic worth compared to others who may not. It preys upon the hope that if one's clothing is a highly regarded brand name, people will have the same elevated regard for you. It purports and hopes to say that if you wear this brand name on your clothing, you will think that you will be seen as a more desirable human being. You do not buy the visible brand so you can see it. You buy it so others will see it.

Brand advertising on blue jean trousers with the label you can't miss, says I'm wearing stuff that costs. I have money, respect me. It's all about seeking approval of your personal being, improving your desirability.

We are immersed all day long in this seeking of being desired by our fellow humans. It's clearly basic in our nature.

This same dynamic is heavily at work in our choice of automobiles. It is also true of how we select and build our houses, and use current fashion to make them our homes. It is what drives people into Facebook, and other social Internet media.

So while no one talks about this directly, you have experienced enough to sit back and connect the dots - and know what is really going on with us humans. Any cool eyed observer will see and know.

Imagine this: If a guy from Mars, the red planet, came down to find out how we humans spend our time living on this planet, what do you think would be his Report back to home base on Mars?

It wouldn't be a complicated Report. it would say that we do survival things to keep us alive: Getting food, housing, and health requirements done, doing it ourselves, or getting jobs servicing each others' wants in order to to earn money to give to others to provide our survival needs to us.

After this, the Report would say, that we then spend all the rest of our waking hours in our lives, creating relationships with each other - meaning getting our individual personal selves to be desired by other humans and expressing our own desire and approval to other humans of their personal existence. The French, with usual directness, have a saying that expresses this so well: "It's not your fault that I love you."

We do everything imaginable to make our bodies look attractive - cosmetics, clothes, perfume, exercise to perfect shape. We incessantly talk to each other 24/7 by devices overcoming any distance. We write. We dance. We sing. We buy and build - all this with an eye to enhance our "desirability" by other people. All for this same purpose - to enhance our relationships of being desired by each other.

In final analysis, what our lives are about is what we do about other people. It is what we do in responding to the people we live with - what we do in relating to them. After survival needs are met, our lives are then all about relationships with other human persons - seeking and holding relationships. The relationships may be sought to increase wealth, but in the end this effort is also related to having our existence further honored and approved by more humans.

So then on Mars, after delivering this Report, they would ask why do these humans do this? What makes them do this? Do they have to? The answer on Mars would probably be: "we don't know - we're working on it, but there is no doubt that this is what these Earth humans do."

This imaginary dialogue is useful. It's a way to step back to a celestial point and look at ourselves from an all embracing distance - and comprehend the real nature of what we humans actually do with our aliveness on this planet.

So "why" do we do all these things? What does this say about the nature of our thoughts? Well, this could take a different kind of understanding. Acquiring an understanding of non-material reality is not teachable. This kind of understanding can only be acquired as a consequence of being actively sought by a person as an act of his free will, an act of self direction.

For a human person, the actual seeking of such understanding is the only way to have the power to understand.

Wisdom thru the ages have told us that no effort at seeking it ever fails and goes unrewarded - one of human life's great secrets. These thoughts are on display in global literature current and ancient, but so few people ever "get" it.

BOTTOM LINE-

So what do the people who do not know you, want from you?

One by one, each of them want you to use your free will to desire their existence, to want them to be.

The words honor, respect and love all mean the same thing when another person understands you are willing and wanting and choosing to desire their being, their existence, their being alive.

One by one, every person wants you to look at them and recognize them as an individual person whose existence is wholeheartedly acknowledged and desired by you.

This basic desire is that nuclear fire in a person that never goes out, never ceases.

This is more easily understood when you conclude from all this discussion that everyone absolutely wants you at a minimum to immediately respect them - meaning showing and giving respect to them individually.

So this is your never-to-fail position in first meeting anyone - when you come to that first moment of mutual awareness - you express your respect towards this individual, by your words or your body language, a friendly nod of the head.

This first movement is ingrained in many cultures as absolutely required, particularly Japanese. Failure to perform acts showing respect leads to instant hostility. Lacking a cultural requirement, you should work on having your personal style of any first meeting, be to create an act showing respect.

As a practical matter, once this understanding becomes part of your own unspoken mindset, it should enable you to approach people for the first time without apprehension. You will have an attitude of already knowing the basic and underlying direction of their life's energy.

Knowing this intimacy about the inside of a person, creates in you the confidence of certainty in approaching any human person.

This confidence eases anxiety, and creates calmness.

Your calm approach wards off hostility, and offers the inviting presumption of personal empathy, without intrusive demands.

Simply said, when you approach people with an attitude that says simply "I am glad you exist", you are then reaching out and touching this born-with yearning in everyone.

It makes it almost impossible for anyone to resist and not genuinely welcome your approach and your personal relationship.

Chapter 6

Intelligent People - Who are They?

How do you know if the people you meet are usefully smart

Have you ever deliberately thought about it? Probably not. What is it that you are trying to say when - off hand - you call somebody smart, or intelligent?

Heading out into the world, this understanding should be part of your baseline thinking. Basic equipment. You should have a clear, clean cut idea about what makes a person intelligent - someone worthy of your reliance.

First of all, intelligent about what? We are not talking here about mathematics or science. We are talking about the central intelligence involved in conducting a human life.

This is the intelligence involved in successfully managing to live with each other.

Living means varying personalities turning to each other, engaging each other, exposing themselves to an exchange of energies, in the pursuit of getting our fellow humans to do what is needed. And in being so engaged, we are talking about the intelligence that can then successfully foresee and forecast outcomes in our dealings with each other.

This is the intelligence that is required for the success of ninety percent of our living activity during our time on this planet.

In sum, it is the intelligence required of what we spend most of our lives doing - relating to people. Creating friendships, and avoiding hostility, or persuading people to perform in any organized effort, or buy what we are selling, is all relating to people.

This critical and highly prized "living intelligence" is not summed up by praising some one who has a lot of facts, easily recalled. A lot of folks are facile with facts, but being quick in reciting facts, is not being intelligent. It's just means having a hard drive in your head, with a decent retrieval rate.

Real intelligence has to do with how you sort out a fact's relationship to other facts.

Anyone can become acquainted with facts. All your life you will be meeting people who have several college degrees, and read three books a week, and can swamp you with their recital of "facts". But somehow you still see them as "boneheads", being very naive in making judgments about people and dealing with the real world.

You need more than "facts" to see what is coming. You have to put the facts in context of how every thing and every one will react to their presence.

It is possible for people to undergo a fact education way beyond their level of intelligence to deal with such facts. So there are a lot of people who are educated beyond their capacity for awareness.

A high level of Intelligence should never be confused with a high level of information.

Excellence in knowing facts is just a component of intelligence. Intelligence comprises information, but it is more than that.

Intelligence is a state of awareness. It is a state of predictive awareness.

Awareness is information on fire. That fire is a burning, never ending effort by a human person striving to see how things relate, how facts will cause consequences, and when related, provide reliable predictions of probable outcomes and consequences needed to be avoided or embraced.

Intelligence is this directed energy imposed on facts - discerning how they will actually relate to possible consequences. This is predictive awareness. This is what intelligence means.

Is a person intelligent? If a person simply showers facts on you, the answer is most probably not.

But if issues are discussed directly in terms of relating facts to the possibilities of performance by individually acting persons, the answer is probably yes.

There is a nexus here, The most important facts that have to be intelligently handled, are facts about individual people. This is true because the most problems that arise in this world are a problem of people behavior.

Predicting this behavior and dealing with it will indeed occupy the bulk of our time and effort in our post childhood world. There is one sure way of telling who is intelligent in these efforts, and who is not.

Those whose awareness compels them to see people problems in terms of the specific individual persons involved, these are the people you should deal with, and recognize as the most usefully intelligent,

Those who easily talk about a people problem chiefly in terms of a group and their characteristics, these are the folks to be avoided as being limited and unaware of individuals, and therefore, a nuisance when trying to solve a "people problem". People are not a problem. Human individuals are, one by one. And it is in understanding and predicting specific and relevant individual behavior that is the hallmark of the highest living intelligence in a human person.

So if there is anything that will distinguish you as a savvy, smart-aware person, it is your persistence in driving discussions to understand the personal nature of the individuals involved in any problem situation.

Seeking this kind of knowledge, is the awareness trait that marks the successful CEOs of any business, big or small.

This awareness, this effective grasp of any problem involving people, is accomplished only by diving in and getting to know and assess the individuals involved, one by one.

This drive Is the essence of awareness that is possessed by persons with "living intelligence". Look for it in persons you want to depend on.

And when you see it, that is a person with whom to join forces. These are persons whose natural focus is to interpret the world by digging into and evaluating the thinking of individual persons - one by one. These are the people you want to work with,

During a period of teaching at a Graduate School of Business, our MBA program included visits and discussions with senior executives of major companies. All of them were CEOs - chief executives officers. Some were retired. I prompted one of my students to ask each of the no longer operating executives, this question: Could look back and see anything that they should have done better, and for which they had regrets in not providing more of their efforts and attention.

The uniformity of their answers was instructive.

It was striking that almost every one of these CEOs mentioned the same reflection: that they should have spent more time in knowing and evaluating their senior people, in their hiring and in assigning their objectives.

In other words, these CEOs are looking back, and wishing they had given more careful thought to understanding the individuals to whom they had given responsibility. They obviously were thinking of disappointments that could have been avoided had they concentrated more to be aware of individual characteristics.

This says something significant. Put yourself in their place. Consider yourself as understanding the pressure and hustle of handling all the varied engines of activity in a major corporation. Then consider, when all is said and done, you as CEO look back and reflect that you should have spent more time on personnel than operations, as a more effective and valuable use of your time. This is a telling judgment. This is a solid core observation of a person who has achieved living intelligence. This should be you.

So when you are asking yourself whether a person is intelligent, the answer will be in whether he or she has and shows this kind of "individual person" oriented awareness that clearly focuses on the relationship of the individual to consequences he or she can cause.

The intelligence you are really looking for, is in the search for this predictive awareness.

Let this be your criteria in understanding the intelligent quotient, the real IQ of the people affecting your world.

Finding and recognizing and having such intelligently aware people by your side, will give you the greatest help in any success you seek. It will be your solid guard against mistakes and mishaps.

Chapter 7

The Clear Grasp of Youth
You Do Not Want to Lose

The Directness of Individual Perception

This is about something you do naturally as a kid, but you get pressured to avoid as an adult. This is about keeping forever a key and keen insight - a perception dimension that you have naturally as a young person.

When you see things go wrong as a young kid, you see two possible reasons: It is either the fault of some uncontrollable physical natural event, or someone screwed up. And as a kid, you are quick to state what you see, when things go wrong, and say what you see as the cause.

Even ancient writings note the astonishing directness with which kids will declare what they see. "Out of the mouths of babes and sucklings" is the well known biblical reference to this.

But young kids simply blurting out and naming the individuals that are to blame, often results in their being dismissed as a young voice to be ignored, or being silenced for starting an undesired discussion.

When you get older, you will find caution is in the air to your naming individuals. There is an awareness of you possibly creating a hostile response. Your naming of individuals you see at fault, is repressed and avoided. You will be asked not to get "personal" in your evaluations, and you will be advised to confine your criticisms to policy and process, as if this is where the problem could only be.

You will often face an insistence on avoiding uncomfortable personal confrontations as a fear induced priority - whatever the problem may be.

It is this social repression of your awareness of specific individuals as being a precise source of things gone wrong, that is the problem we want to note here. People do not want to face the likely hostile response from naming out loud the individuals at fault.

This fear of personal confrontation in the adult world will attack the fresh direct sensibilities of your youth, and discourage your truthful perceptions.

As you grow older, you will find yourself increasingly intimidated to not speak freely of your understanding of individuals at fault. So you will slow down your speaking out loud - because you don't want trouble.

In time, this slowing down will dull your appetite to deal with the truth - unless you somehow boldly and consciously decide that you will not let this youthful and bare knuckle grip on reality slide away. But it comes off like a soft glove. And it is tugged at when you are not paying attention.

So It won't be easy to keep. There are a lot of forces to dull your sense of an individual centered world of how things happen - not just fear of public confrontation with individuals at fault.

Modern education will certainly tone you down. From tenth grade thru college -from age 16 to 21 and onwards - history courses, sociology courses, and even literature courses will teach the view that peoples' individual behavior can be explained by great economic or social conflicts and changes. All of this may or may not be true. You never really know how an individual is affected by anything, until that individual tells you.

But from a student's point of view, these macro (great) events become the imposed and accepted explanation and interpretation of specific conduct by individuals. With this thinking, it is implied that no further discussion or research is necessary to confirm what an individual might have actually thought about how these events might have affected his life. As a student you just accept the big picture explanation in place of not really having any evidence from the concerned individuals as to how they were actually affected.

Modern education run students through reams of these big picture explanations. You get it in high school, and this thematic education is a major activity in college.

But all this may have a strange consequence for you after school when you meet the real world.

No matter what you're doing, you will be in people management on some basis. You will be predicting people behavior. You will be encountering general propositions of about people why they are thinking and how they are affected, just as you did in college or high school. And without more, just as you did in school, you will assume that the general propositions are at operative way for you to think about and deal with individuals described to you in generalized explanations - in your every day world.

This falsely accepts that to understand the truth about people, there is no need to be aware of individuals' actual thinking and conduct, one on one.

So just as you did in school, you easily go from a generalized statement about people that is fed to you, to imposing its belief on the concerned individuals that you must deal with now in your life.

This is where your education has not done you a favor. In the real world, you have to inevitably deal with people as individuals one by one. You have to get your head out of the academic world.

The only way to know the reality of an individual is in studying and knowing persons precisely as individuals, one by one. This is hard to do. So it is avoided as a task. The academic way of using generalizations is much easier and more comfortable. So getting down to the individual level is avoided as a task - if you let your education guide you.

In school, we are asked to be comfortable with speculation in big picture generalizations, and let the summary generalizations be the reliable story of real individuals in what actually occurs in their lives as a result of any large event they are said to experience.

From the generalized studies you are given in your education you are led and told to infer what has been the actual conduct of individuals.   It should be the other way around.

We should best come to generalizations only from the study of individuals. But you can be educated to go forward in operating your life by defining individuals from the speculation of generalizations. This is where truth gets lost in this reverse flow thinking.

This is just another example of how some schooling can dull you down. If you kept your kid wits about you, you would be skeptical of accepting this. - because you have no real evidence of individuals' thinking being presented to you. You would only see the reality here of an individual's conduct as only being inferred, as just a logical guess. In the last analysis, this is just speculation derived from big picture sociology and history courses.

So be cautious about letting your education cut your use of your own street smarts in striving to know individuals as the solid ground for your decisions.

The problem to note then is this: when you get exposed to too much generalization in your studies, and you let your indulgence in academic study and speculation replace your kid sharp sense for wanting to know the actual truth about individuals, you lose it.

You lose your youthful affinity for zeroing in on individuals when discussing people, evaluating their conduct - which is something you must be doing at some point in every day of your life.

Zeroing in on the play of individuals should be your life long way of understanding how bad things happen - in the historical past as well as in the present. It is also the basis for understanding how good things happen.

The most effective CEO's understand this. They don't interpret problems as mere policy conflicts or protocols to be adjusted. They zero in to how things happened, individual by individual.

Never lose this inscape, which is so often ignored by highly educated people in favor of studies and analyses. Business how-to books are written to show off new theories with catchy labels declaring how things work and providing formula and protocols for solutions. But they seldom mention the root of human organization problems, the tangle with the failings and ambitions of errant individuals, one by one.

So throughout your life, you should tell yourself that you will insist on seeing how things happen as a consequence of individuals acting one by one. This must remain your deliberate approach, defining the street smart and individually oriented person you are now - in your youth.

You will undertake to know exactly how things happen by envisioning specific individuals acting, second by second. This should be your lifetime MO (modus operandi - a Latin phrase meaning the way you operate, and analyze what's going on). This is your personal standard for what constitutes reality in human affairs.

Persistent pursuit along this road, insisting on minute detail of individuals involved in any troubling situation, is the only effort worth making. No detail is too small. Having this detailed knowledge is what distinguishes the confident CEOs of business enterprises, large or small, who really know what is going on.

This is the approach that lets an employer understand, for instance, whether an employee's failure is actually the employer's failure - failure to instruct clearly.

Following this MO, is really necessary, if you want to be the kind of person that is on top of every situation in which you are involved.

Getting involved in the commercial world is inevitable for most of you. Doing "deals", participating in dealmaking is in your future. Tons of books have been written to give advice on deal making, and how to negotiate. Great advice, like great truths, is never complicated. It all comes down to discerning the context in which each individual involved is thinking.

Doing deals – think personally.
Deals are all about individuals. Know each involved individual's situational awareness.
Deals are about content and credibility.
Credibility is about the individual person, and your capability of understanding his trust worthiness.

Your deals are going to be as good as your ability to make an assessment of the individuals making deals with you. You shrewdly put yourselves in their shoes.

But in trying to carry this remarkable focus into adult years, young people also encounter a natural inhibition that comes with doing something really strange for them. Young people are only used to zeroing in on individuals that occupy their familiar life in their growing up years. They don't bother to close in on people they don't know, that don't belong to their personal world.

So as you begin your becoming years and immerse yourself in the impersonal world, this must change. As a youth it was easy and natural for you to put yourself in the shoes of someone you do know well, and figure out how they would feel or react to now or future events. Because practically everybody you knew in growing up, you knew well.

As a young person, you are not used to getting up close and personal to people you do not know well. So it is uncomfortable for you to think about entering the personal world of particular people you don't already really know.

You will just have to make this new kind of effort, to successfully dwell in this world's impersonal forest. Unlike what you have done in the past, you now have to make the unfamiliar effort to stand in the shoes of people you barely know, and figure out where their heads are at, or will be at, when confronting events you know are likely to happen. So you think it thru and envision individual by individual reaction to what they are likely to be dealing with. And you prepare.

You will be surprised at how much you can know about individuals if you just stand still and make this effort of standing in their shoes, and think of how things would be seen thru their eyes, their personality. It will bring together your passing observations that you may have never focused on.

In the wilds beyond your growing-up world, this focus on understanding individuals is how you predict, and this is how you create awareness.

And this focused awareness is what will make you smart and effective, and keep you out of unfortunate entanglements, and have you way ahead of other people in smartly predicting outcomes.

Bottom line:

Learn to see yourself standing in the shoes of other people, and looking at the world from their viewpoint as you try to understand what they see and feel.

In your times to come, you will see this as the key to all successful operations involving people. And the things that we do on this earth that do not involve people, are very few and far between.

A guiding principle then: Examine every problem in an analysis of the individuals involved. Drilling down on these individuals should be your strength, your modus operandi (MO), your own way of operating in a state of maximum awareness. Ultimately, this will be your strength. This is how you will get things done.

And go into every situation new to you, by focusing on the kind and quality of the individuals involved. This acute initial awareness of the new individuals around you, will give you quickly a dominate perspective. It will mean you are doing this sharp focus on all individuals around you as a conscious deliberate act. This should happen.

This is the definition of being 'street smart'. You focus on the individual, you search to know by standing in another person's sandals. These are the questions you ask in wondering how 'street smart' you are, as well as the people around you.

Chapter 8

WHO ARE YOU?

You are not the Horse you ride

BETWEEN 18 and 28, this will begin to happen: every person newly met will pointedly ask you what's your occupation?

And, if not a student, you will come with the answer, saying I am an accountant, a lawyer, a software engineer, or engaged in a task for a certain company.

Just chit chat? More often it's more pointed. The person asking would just like to know if you're someone that needs respect and caution. So your answer by habit should also be instinctively cautious.

You should not open yourself for judgment by just describing your job. You are not to be disposed of by simply describing your daily tasks.

You ride an economic horse. That horse is named and called by what you do for a living. But you are not the horse. And you should make a point of this.

You are so much more than the horse you ride.

So consciously deal with this. Don't let yourself be defined by your day job, whatever it is.

Let's say that you finally finished law school, and passed the required exam to get your license to practice law. You meet someone at a party. Conversation is slow. And so the normal question is asked inquiring about what you do. Your prideful answer is: "We'll, I am a lawyer." But an honestly real answer would be this: I work at being me. Being a lawyer is the horse I ride." You won't say this. But it should be your attitude in letting people know that you are more than what you do.

You want to give some leadership to the people you newly meet, in how you want them to think about you.

The vision of yourself that you want to present to others, or even to your own consciousness, should go beyond a framed picture of your daily work.

You are always more, much more than what you do to source money. So while you ride an economic horse, you are not the horse.

When people want to find out who you are, you do not want to be a mystery easily solved. Keep it that way.

The young crowd, age 18 to 28 particularly feel anxious to tell people that they are an engineer, or a TV producer, or any labeled recognized job they have, as a point of pride seeking approval. There is no stopping this. But doing it in a restrained, consciously modest manner, will suggest there is more to your person than this labelled job.

So indulge in this pointed truth with a touch of class: Never let yourself be summed up by the title to your job. What you think is a touchstone for instant respect, can just as easily be an occasion for your dismissal. You never know how people will relate to your employment. It can be instant disgust, as easily as instant respect.

A mere statement of the label of your occupation will connect to a listener's preconceived idea of the qualities of the person with that occupation - something that you will know nothing about. It could be stature enhancing or the opposite. So letting your job label be used as your introduction, could unwittingly dim and diminish your prospects for being considered as a person with other possibilities, in other lights.

Bottom line: when asked about your occupation, try to respond in a manner that is low key - meaning show restraint and indifference - and give resistance to letting other people sum you up by your job description.

Labeling yourself with your job, is a temptation invited by the very young. They are keen on letting people know they really do have an accomplishment status. Why? Because they never had a status before in growing-up. Why? Well, basically all that anyone is able to do in growing-up is grow up. It is a full time project.

But what is the actual harm in now touting yourself by way of describing your economic status - your job?

Allowing your job to be an initial summing of you, can immediately put off the possibility of a real relationship, and diminish interest in you as a person.

Don't block anyone's view of you, by putting your resume in their face.

As a person, you should always loom larger than your current job or profession.

So be coy about letting yourself be occupation labeled. Downplay it, no matter how proud you are.

You really want to be fully known and addressed as the wonderfully complicated and multifaceted person you know you are. This takes time. Don't let it be cut short by touting a job label.

You're a person, not an occupation.

Chapter 9

A KEYHOLE TO UNDERSTANDING PERSONALITY

Look for the Organizing Power of Fear

After 18, you will be meeting a greater number of people new to you, than you ever did in your earlier years.

You should meet them with a new mindset, that reflects your evolving status in the world.

A kid's "hi there" greeting, can no longer be the brief activity of your meeting.

When - now - you first meet a new person, and make your first eye contact with your out reached hand, this will be the beginning of some shrewd and further thinking on your part.

You will be looking for answers about the people you meet. Because now you have reasons for questions. You will be meeting them on your own terms, no longer being a protected child.

After 18, you are on a more equal basis with people than you were as a kid. There will be a higher level of mutual awareness. You should always anticipate that you may be getting into an unspoken relationship of some kind that involves "what am I going to do about you, and what are you going to do about me."

Instinctively, you will be wanting to know more about new people confronting you - particularly if you know you may be having a continuing relationship.

So you should deliberately create for yourself a particular new mindset in meeting new people, after you reach 18, and begin your becoming years.

First thing, put your mind fully in gear when meeting new persons. Be attentive. I would like to say: explode into attentiveness, without appearing to go overboard. Just be very focused when first meeting another person. First meetings are remembered.

A new mindset for meeting people is not going to require having answers - the right answers. It is going to require having questions - the right questions.

Basically there is only one question to ask a human being - the only living things on this planet that have a free will. Simply - what do you want?

This is important. Because having a free will, you, as a human, can want anything. As a dog, you would by nature be really restricted to wanting things that only dogs can use. As a human, there is no such restriction on what you can want.

The full honest answer to this question to a human, "what do you want", will tell you everything about the life they are living.

But the question to a person as to what they want, is definitely not a simple question. Because there is a telling part of what any person wants that has to be separated out in terms of why is it desired.

There are things you desire in terms of avoiding something, and those you desire to acquire something.

The things you want to avoid, are generally the most powerful desires in all the range of your wanting. These are things you would further describe as fears. The things you fear are your most powerful and persistent and immediately present desires. Fears are desires of avoidance that override the desires to acquire.

So- more than anything else, the first thing you want to know about a person, is what are the scope of his fears - what he does not want. This will tell you more about a person, then knowing about some one's aspirational goals. There is a reason for this. It is because fears relate to your core instincts for survival. Your fears ride that horse. Survival is the core energy that drives every living thing. And your fears demand a "now" response.

Traditionally, when we think about a person's wants, we think about their goals that are happily sought, not about their fears.

But your fears by their nature are always claiming and seeking priority attention. They seep into every corner of your personality. They are underfoot in every choice. They surround you like elevator music. They are the hidden nudge in your every decision.

So knowing what fears a person has, or what fears he doesn't have, is a major key to understanding anyone's personality.

But fears are not just about avoiding undesirable circumstances. Fears are also about attitudes. How a person reacts, for instance, when he is frustrated and holds a fearing preoccupation with worry over not immediately obtaining what is desired. Knowing how a person handles frustration is knowing part of their fear system. It is a key to understanding what world of fear a person is living in.

Walking through a person's hall of fears, is the most effective way to understanding that person.

So the most important question you will have of a person you are meeting and wanting to know, is the question of what he wants in terms of what he fears.

This is the one fundamental blank you want to fill in: What does this individual fear? What mindset of fears does this person possess? Because fear, where ever built into a person, is the master organizing principle that significantly controls and dominates every aspect of a personality.

People's personalities are ultimately defined and driven by the makeup and pattern of whatever personal fears are present, and just as importantly, not present.

Fear will control the choice of careers, control their judgments and risk taking. And fundamentally their mindset of fear will control their social life, whether they are an outgoing person that reaches easily to embrace other people, or a person withdrawn or hesitant to address themselves to others.

Fear, if anywhere present, will be the organizing principle of these choices - the controlling dynamic.

Fear is a heavy presence. It can be the consequence of genetic inheritance or be induced by a life's unfortunate experiences.

Wherever present in a personality, it has the persistent organizing power of a hurricane that won't go away. It rides with that unquenchable force for survival inherent in every living thing. This is what makes it so powerful and so central to one's personality.

The ingrained presence of fear will control the overall character of anyone's personality.

Fear is the constant anticipation of undesirable consequences - consciously or unconsciously.

Many personalities are primarily organized around fear. It is a coloring mindset. It is exactly like a filter put on the front end of a camera lens. It controls the character of light that flows thru the camera from start to finish.

If your wondering whether a person is capable of bold innovation, thinking in new ways to solve problems, you would consider whether you are dealing with a mindset that is fear sensitive. If you see a fearing personality, and a lifestyle of avoiding risk, you have your answer. Such a person should not be expected to deal well with tasks requiring new big changes.

The current thinking is that the mindset of fearing begins in infants, and is in large part genetically based - as is about 60 percent of personality formation. It is nature being recognized now as the dominant cause over nurture of hard core personality traits. The other way around, of nurture dominating nature as the leading cause of personality formation, was the largely accepted doctrine taught as recently as the 1960's.

You will never know an individual, until you understand his or her fear-set. So when you meet another person whom you want to know, this should automatically be your first point of wonder. Train yourself to focus this as a conscious question, and clues to the answer will fall into place. A focusing effort always has astonishing results.

Fear is so fundamental a driving force in human living, that you can actually see people's lives divide and organize according to its intrusive quality. Here is one way of generally describing how fear organizes people into distinguishing traits:

There are cave people. There are hilltop people. Then there are people we can only call "orbitors." People in orbit who want, who demand to be involved in the whole show of existence.

The cave people, we have all met. They are in the majority. They are folks who prefer living in a cave. Caves provide maximum safety. They live their lives primarily seeking protection, and security and certainty. They will not be pushed out of the security of their cave. They will call this their comfort zone. They do not want to be moved, improved, or enticed to experiment.

The hilltop people are a somewhat rarer breed. They definitely do not want to live in a cave. They want to see all that's going on. They want to live on a hill top, where they can see all. Protection and security will be dealt with when necessary. They are not interested in organizing their lives around anticipating problems and fears. They want the freedom to know all, and they are not inclined to let fearing things interfere.

But the most uninhibited fear-free folks, are the orbiters. Mentally, and spiritually in their view, they are circling the earth, as outliers. They want to know absolutely everything, see everything. Not willing to be tied down by belonging to any fixed point, they are ultimate existentialists. Whatever is, they want the freedom to know it. There are not many of these around. They are this way from birth - fearless. But they often pay the price that comes with a lack of attention to risk. You will know them when you see them. They are full force human beings.

Bottom Line:

You should know people in terms of how they fear. Why? You will know the limits of what you can ask them to do in the normal course of living. You will understand the limits of what they can be expected to do on an everyday basis. These are the limits that have to be respected in your ongoing relationship with them.

Keep an eye on the limits of the people around you in terms of their fears. You will get nowhere trying to change them. Deal with them as they are. Fearful people have self imposed leashes.

Focusing on people's fears will make you street smart.

You will want to note Individuals driven by a fear mindset. It will be important for you to recognize them, as you get along in life. Fear thoughts and attitudes take precedence in most people's thinking. They will accommodate their fear mindset rather than grab the bull by the horns in solving any problem. For this reason, fear prone people make useless problem solvers, and worse leaders. Being street smart, you will recognize this, and avoid your involvement,

Don't try to cut anything tied to an individual's sense of survival - be it physical or personal. You can more easily change what people find attractive, than what people fear.

So take time, take a moment, and directly ask yourself about any individual in front of you, and with whom you have a significant working relationship: What are the personal fears of this person I am relying upon? The answer will have you forewarned.

Just asking the question within your own mind will give you thoughtful, useful reflections. You will make yourself more aware about the life you are living.

Your life is about the people around you.

Chapter 10

SELF ESTEEM - A reality twisted

Do I have sufficient self-esteem? How would I know? Any ideas? Anyone?

This is a secret question that afflicts so many young persons as they tackle the impersonal world. There are all kinds of perspectives to answer the self esteem question. Here is one perspective that takes a close look in a practical way. It rings true. See if you don't agree.

How can you really know what self esteem means - to you? The concern for self-esteem is very popular. You are supposed to know.

But it has never been very clear about what you are supposed to understand in thinking about your self esteem - when you can say you have it, or when you do not. So most young people just ignore the whole subject. Anyway, it sounds depressing.

But it is not good to kick any idea out of your garage without looking at it.

And when you do look closely at self esteem, you will find yourself looking at a crazy turtle on its back, pawing the air for traction.

You will see this self esteem idea is some kind of upside down thinking. You will realize that you have to turn it on its head, to know what it is.

Consider yourself alone in the desert - just by yourself - puzzling with no success over a textbook on calculus that you tried and tried, but could not understand. Noting your failure, would you find yourself embarrassed in your frustration, sitting there on the hard sand by your lonesome self?

Would you be having a fit over a loss of self respect, also known as a loss of self esteem, because you are not understanding this calculus stuff? You are reading it over and over. But is still not clear to you. Are you sitting there in the sun, just red-faced with embarrassment?

Doubtful. Sitting by your lonesome self, you would just drop it for another day.

But if you were not alone, and your companions by your side were going successfully from one calculus lesson to the next, you could not casually put your lesson book down in frustration. Failing in front of people is a different story.

You would be conscious of your failure being seen by your companions. You will be in anguish, and you will be squirming as you become conscious that other people are watching and knowing that you are stumbling while they are succeeding.

You would only feel worse if your failure was over more personal stuff than calculus, such as not doing well in sport competition, and social relationships, where everybody is aware that everybody is watching you.

In an instant moment of self reflection, you are seeing yourself in the thoughts of other people - their consciousness of your failings.

It is in such a moment of self reflection - of yourself reflected in other people's eyes - that you come to what is popularly known as a loss of self esteem.

So you come to understand that self-esteem is to be defined as your own conscious awareness of other people's diminished assessment of you, where you see yourself as undesirable in their eyes.

But why is other peoples' lesser opinion of you so self shriveling and depressing? Why do you suddenly want to hide yourself under a rock - in instinctive defense? When all that has happened is simply this: your mind has acquired an idea about what is in somebody else's head? Why do you really care what is in somebody else's head?

Before answering that, let's make this immediate observation. Your self esteem becomes only an issue when you view yourself in the context of experiencing other people around - you real or imagined.

Living alone in a desert, you would never have a self esteem problem. It requires people around you, who are conscious of you. It requires you to be conscious of their awareness of you. And it further requires your noting that they are holding a view of your self as being undesirable and deserving disapproval. Together these are the only conditions (short of mental illness) in which a loss of self esteem can occur.

So in observing this, you come to understand that your "self esteem" problem is better termed as your "other people esteem of you" problem.

When you hear the words "self-esteem", you now know that the esteem of your self is not the problem. It is your acceptance of any low esteem that you see other people have towards you, that is the problem.

It is other people's mindset towards you, that is upsetting you, not your own mindset towards yourself.

So why do you really care what is in somebody else's head?

They are the problem. Not yourself, unless you are just imagining other people's thoughts that do not really exist.

You get this lack of respect not from your own thinking generated by yourself, as the self-esteem preachers have long promoted. You get it from thinking about other people who are thinking about you. You get it from your own perception that there are people around you, who are thinking about their lower approval of you because of something that you have not done well.

So when and if you ever get the feeling of being beaten down by feelings of being personally inadequate, just pause and think it through. Be honest with yourself and see whether your sinking feelings are really not about yourself, but about other people thinking badly about you. Call this out to yourself clearly.

And when you acknowledge that it is other people's thinking and attitude towards you that is the problem, then face this, and be clear to yourself about what you are seeing.

If you see that they are disrespecting the total person you are, because, for example, you don't get calculus easily, did not perform a task well, then your dealing with their judgment about you, should be straight forward.

If their thinking about you is truthful, then be honest about your self. Deal with the truth you know. And do not be afraid of letting people know you are doing so. Being honest about one's self, absolutely compels people's respect.

You should care about other people's low opinion of you, only if it is based on some truth.

If it is not, then the shoe is on the other foot. You have reason to hold them in low esteem for having an untruthful idea, a careless, thoughtless view of you.

But either way, you know this: You know there is infinitely more to you as a person and your existence then getting an understanding of calculus and it's conceptual configurations, or doing praise-catching moves in team sports, or having envious social relationships. There is so much more to you. But why should anyone agree with your own honest self assessment, if you don't think it first.

Don't be quick to consider yourself deficient. People who are unreasonably critical of you can actually be the ones with the ultimate problem of defective thinking - about you. And you have the obligation to grab onto your own force of life and with truth understand how to dismiss their diminishing thinking about yourself.

To do this you have to attend to your own thinking . What should you think, when faced with very wrong and very unfair comments about yourself? How do you handle it? What are you supposed to think in response to unfair, untrue criticism?

This is a life long issue. Here is where you separate the calm and self-possessed grown-ups from the still hapless, easily disturbed kids who have yet to figure out how in truth to respond to unfair criticism.

This is a big topic. You should tackle this right now when you are young. For your present and future happiness, lay out now your own clear and calm thinking on dealing with the confrontations that will happen to you - in your living with humans holding a free will.

And this is the next chapter.

Chapter 11

When will you know that you have grown-up?

- a Test -

Almost all who have entered the forest of impersonal humans, like you, first wandering thru after age 18, have been amazed at the human beings they have encountered.

Looking back after awhile, most folks will tell you it has been a somewhat awesome experience -   that can be surprisingly summarized:

"People are worse than you know, and better than you have ever dreamed."

The "better than you have ever dreamed" experience, will reward your adventure in meeting new people, in ways you may have yet to imagine.

In coming to know really good persons, your life experiences a glow you never forget. Discovering such a personality makes the world the place you want to be and belong.

But meanwhile, what will take more of your time and energy, is the "worse than you know" part. You will experience people who will deeply disturb you with displays of bad conduct and intentions that are clearly beyond your experience in growing up.

How you, as a young person, will handle this rude and jolting experience is of concern to everyone who cares about you. It is when you are first confronted and shocked with a deliberate, uncaring, undeserved and wanton injury given to you by another human being, that you actually lose your innocence. This is when you discover the dicey world of destructive humans among which you must live. No escape.

For your own protection, thinking ahead, you will want to be prepared for people problems you never thought possible.

So how do the best among us on this planet, prepare to handle a personal assault coming unexpectedly out of an everyday world from people? How do the best level headed people among us, deal with the unfair criticism, the unexpected betrayal, the unwarranted shoving aside, the being ignored?

The best among us will have taken the time to understand something that creates a very steady distinctive grip on human reality which keeps them from being caught up in a preoccupation of outrage when undeserved assault comes their way.

That something is a clear grasp of an explanation for crazy awful human conduct, when all other explanations fail, and when you are honest in knowing that nothing you did could have reasonably caused it. No mental illness is apparent. No genetic tendencies are a likely reason.

This something is a bottom line explanation and answer that consciously looks at every individual human person we will ever deal with, and accepts that there is something special that is present in human persons that exists nowhere else in Nature.

That something is the free will that each person possesses - meaning the human person is actually free to do, or to say, or to desire absolutely anything, with or without reason. This power is peculiar.

It is best understood by noting that other living things, not human, do not have this power. Animals and plants do not. The on going energies in nature do not. Stars and galaxies do not have this power. Except for human persons, every thing else existing around you, can only desire and do and be what they are.

In this world, Humans are the only living things that you will ever experience that can choose to be what they are not.

Human persons are free to chose any conduct - whether it reflects the truth of their existence or not.

So here should be a lifelong stabilizing focus - an anchor point: That the most honest, most useful grip on human reality is your accepting acknowledgment of every person's actual free will - to commit any act or think any thought. There doesn't have to be a reason.

Humans, unlike anything else in the natural world, can and will do anything, and sometimes for no other reason than because they can - meaning no reason. In the old biblical allegorical tale of human beginnings, Adam admitted he gave the forbidden apple to Eve to eat - why? - because - simply noted -

he could. No reason. It is the towering ego of a human person flashing the free will of his being. He has the power. He can.

Until you are ready and willing to go about living your life with a steady consciousness of this boundless power that human persons possess, you are not grown up. You remain a little kid - still unknowing. You are still able to be bewildered, and be dazed and amazed that people can and will do stupid things, and deliberately hurt you.

But in growing up and becoming solidly conscious of humans' unique possession of free will, you will no longer spend your time in confusion, as to how outrageous, unfair, dishonest, untruthful conduct by your fellow human beings, is possible.

As a fully grown and developed person, you acknowledge that the reality of a human is such that each individual does possess this free will - and that only each individual can control his free will.

There is no other possibility of control - other than having a human's body forcibly imprisoned where his free will is captured as to what he can physically do. You will reflect that we do indeed have prisons for this purpose. Still this is only a partial control in physically restricting a human's body. The mind cannot be restricted.

So this is when you will know that you have arrived at being a mature person among mankind, when you actually see yourself not panicking in reacting to the craziness, the irrationality, of another human being - meaning you no longer wring your hands and find yourself personally confused over the injustice of another person's behavior towards you. You will recognize a free will at work, and if you do not see any practical possibility of correcting persuasion, you turn away to carry on your life.

So you will see yourself understanding this familiar metaphor of response: that "He who stops to kick every barking dog, shall never finish his journey." In other words, if people can behave without reason, there can be no reason to spend a moment of your mind time dwelling on the irrational.

The hardest part of "growing up" is accepting the unrelenting reality that every person you will ever encounter has a free will to act in way you would never think possible, or even dream as probable.

The key word here is "accepting." This doesn't mean you agree with any one's actions. It means you accept this reality about people: a free will is present in every person, one by one, and explains how irrational, dishonest conduct can and does exist.

So you look at every person coming into your field of vision, as a 'free will' coming at you.

Your attitude towards this recognition of individual free will, should be an attitude of respect - in this sense: It should be the same sort of reality respect, we give the stars, gazing at a million of them at night. They just exist. So we give this reality of free will, an honest respect that does not argue about this hard reality existing.

So like the ever present light of stars, we see a free will that lurks and shines in the eyes of all our fellow humans. Similarly we deal with it as being simply real, always there, and not something we can change.

When you have made this consciousness a core part of your awareness, you will know that you have arrived at a calm non-disturbable center for your own life's hurricane of human relationships.

You will have arrived there when your vision understands that you can want people to think in a certain way, but you can never ever force a person to really think and feel as you want. And you understand without quarreling, this is just the way it is with all humans on this planet.

When you make this consciousness of a human's no-limit free will, part of your hand-in-hand daily walk with reality, then you know you are a person with mature awareness, not easily thrown off balance - as will happen when you cannot otherwise explain why other people act irrationally in what they say and do. The stability of your own mind demands an answer.

When you see your own thoughts and reactions reflecting your consciousness of free will, then you will understand that you have grown-up.

Understanding all this is what should cause you to pause and realize that the most dangerous living thing on this planet, is not a hungry bear or a roaring lion. It is a crazy out of control human being who holds a free will.

And if you also pause here, and think of the older people in your life whom you have most trusted and admired, are these not the people who have shown you calmness in adversity? These are people who are not easily startled by the misbehavior of their fellow human beings. They accept the awesome fact that each person does in fact have a free will that can consciously disregard the truth they know. They know they continuously live with this possibility of evil. Because, as you will ultimately come to realize, this is what evil is: The willful disregard of the truth one knows. Only a free will can do this. In biblical lore, this was the ancient understanding of the story of Adam and Eve

Such people, in willful disregard of truth, individuals one by one, will come into your life, and oppose you. Your efforts to deal with them, can just fail. So what do you do? Torture your mind and body with your frustration? Go seething thru months and years contemplating their outrageous behavior?

Instead, you will come down to earth, and recognize that people have a free will on this planet - everyone of them. They can be as crazy and unresponsive as they want. This is what we deal with on this planet,

So now as a younger person, you should put your own thoughts up on the private stage of your mind for your review. Then deliberately recognize that free will is part of your sense of your own reality, and that there is also this free will force in every person you know. You can pause and dwell in the age old discussions about the nature and extent and the why of free will in human beings. But that is not for this moment. Here we want to deal with the factual reality of it's every day intrusion into our lives, and make sure we establish the conscious acknowledgement necessary to adjust to this reality in our every day dealings with the people we encounter.

Consider this: It's an awful contemplation to understand that our parents and best friends whose loyalty and love we have grown to trust, nevertheless could - unthinkably - dump us. Not likely, you say, and you are right to be comfortable. But you do understand that it is the nature of everyone's human reality to have a free will, and so this is possible.

Contemplating the existence of this free will in people close to us, is a lonely place to go. But it is a stark reality. And for their love to be real, their free will is also a necessary reality. You want to understand this.

You must know that you are never truly loved, unless the free will not to do so, also exists. Love can only exist, if it is given by a free will. But free will in being free, the free possibility to do evil, must also exist. A free will is a free will. So if a human being has the power to love with a free will, he is also given the power to do evil, by reason of having that free will.

Hence, we have the great gamble of our reality, that having the possibility to love in our human nature requires that the possibility to do evil also be present.

This huge reality of human beings, each one, having a free will, is difficult to contemplate when we are young. You don't even think about it. But those who have had more years to be involved in thousands of interchanges with the human individual, will have the fact of people's free will in the forefront of their minds more firmly as they accumulate everyday life.

Try to get this understanding when you are young. It is a very maturing effort. You do this by not letting yourself be bent out of shape, when people cause you disaster, cause grave consequences to you, by ignoring what you need, betraying your interests, by refusing to recognize and relate to the truth about you that they can and do know.

Instead of letting such events confuse and destroy you, you will have this poise, this solid understanding of the life you are in, that Individual human persons with free will are free to create their conduct without reason. They can say anything, do anything. They are free to deny the truth they know, to boldly refuse to recognize the truth in front of their face.

In time, you will be able to stare unblinkingly at this very basic fact of human existence.

So as a young person, you will want to have the poise - meaning holding a state of balance - to face and stand up to terrible situations caused by human action, and when it happens, to clearly understand that you are witnessing the exercise of a human's capacity to freely will destruction and denial of what's true and real.

You will want to have this poise, and hold this mental balance of being able to understand what's going on. You are not confused by your distress, and become mentally weakened for lack of an explanation. You will know this is the "free will" peculiar to human reality at work. With this poise, events will never diminish you, as they are likely to do, if you do not understand how or why your fellow humans can cause bad things to happen.

BOTTOM LINE:

You are born. Like it or not, you are faced with the onslaught of human life. Yet in all this, the hardest thing to understand, to actually realize, is that individuals whom you know well and persons you are just meeting, each has a totally free will.

You will never grow up, until you have this in the forefront of your consciousness in all your relating to people.

This is the ultimate poise - the clarity - the cool head - you want, as you put one step ahead of the other, and walk through the crowds of your time.

You will know you have this poise - this quiet acknowledgment of free will in every human person - when you find yourself allowing people not to like you - without lingering resentment. You let it happen without a whimper.

Simply said, you give people permission not to like you. This certainly does not mean you agree with such an attitude. It means you are accepting the reality of individual free will which makes this possible - however irrational it may be.

And when you find yourself able to do this, you have indeed, grown-up.

Chapter 12

Managing Your Mind
The Freedom of Self Direction

Knowing how to think the thoughts
you want

You may not have an urgent need to read this Chapter. But some day you will.

It has to do with being young, and losing your innocence, and handling the aftermath.

Losing your innocence? You will know it when it happens. It has nothing to do with virginity. It has nothing to do with anything good.

It has to do with your first major assault at the hands of another human being, that you did not bring upon yourself - a personal attack that you did not deserve.

As we discussed in the last chapter, you can take such an outrageous personal event in stride, if you already know how it can happen. You have the conscious knowledge that you live surrounded on every side by humans who have a free will to do everything and anything irrational. This is real - not fantasy. And you have already accepted that it can happen - you can be irrationally assaulted.

But there is one problem, that makes this thinking - this explanation - not a solution when trying to avoid being continually troubled after you have been outrageously hurt by another human being's use of his free will.

When you are confronting such conduct that truly and deeply offends you, you cannot help having a strong, near explosive emotional response. When your mind is so seared, your subconscious doesn't forget. Like your body, it cannot ignore the lingering pain of being badly burned. it will replay in your mind, like a TV that cannot be turned off.

Eventually, the events of continuing living, will slow down the reemergence of hurtful memories. You know it is pointless to think about it, but you still do. So how do you stop thinking about it - and quickly?

How do you control your mind? How do you manage your thoughts?

This is a problem for young minds that get assaulted by almost traumatic happenings, and then more often for older people as their memories accumulate.

The answer is to take a moment in your life, and sit down with yourself and consider how - meaning in what manner - your mind, and everyone's, works with memories.

First, you have to view your mind in a radically different way.

Let's assume by age 18, everyone has seen an ocean in movement going back and forth, tossed by every wind that happens to come along. You can see yourself observing this, sitting apart, but not in the water.

Your mind is your own personal and private ocean of memories. You have to learn to sit on its shore, and be an observer.

Your mind, like your body, has a life of its own. It tosses to the surface all that follows any suggestion of an association with a past event that comes from a happening at any moment. Suddenly, an unwanted memory will surface into the daylight of your active thinking. You did not seek its appearance. But there it is, suddenly in front of your mind's vision.

You do not want to deal with it. So how can you get rid of this unwanted memory now in your vision? You have to take two steps: Observe and then Intervene.

First, understand that the mind that is tossing up unwanted memories for your attention, is not you. You are not your mind. You must learn to understand your relationship with your mind. It is much like your relationship with your body. Spurred by your subconscious memory, your mind operates without your direction. It can also operate with your direction. Just like your body can operate, do things, with or without your direction. You are an observer of your body. You know this. So, likewise, you must be an observer of your mind's ocean, sitting by its shore.

Probably no one has ever told you this, growing up - that you have to learn to be an observer of your own mind. It doesn't come up in anyone's everyday conversation. But it should. Because one day you may be really needing this know-how. In dealing with unwanted memories or ideas, you must decisively train yourself to sit as an "observer" over your mind's activities, just like you do with your body. If your body itches, you observe the occurrence. You deal with it. Sometimes for medical reasons you are told not to scratch, but to alleviate the urge by pinching another part of your body. This is intervening.

This replaces, or eradicate one sensation by creating another. To do this effectively takes practice. Practice means having the patience to keep trying - the same patience you know in training your body. This is the same effort for training your mind - your ability to control what your mind deals with. It will require the same practice and patience you give to your body.
.
So with unwanted memories, you eradicate and replace one unwanted thought with another deliberately chosen. You cannot think of two things at once.

So when your mind does bring up an unwanted memory, your reaction is to be an observer saying: "well, there goes my mind again tossing up this unwanted memory to be conscious about."

You learn to confine yourself to take this stance of being an observer - just noting what your mind is doing. Your mind left alone, operates on automatic pilot. It is not you bringing up this memory. It only becomes you when you tolerate it by inaction. So just keep yourself confined to responding as an Observer.

The second step to control unwanted memories is to actively embrace this simple truth that you cannot think of two things at once.

You have experienced this in taking school exams. You cannot be thinking about the answer to an exam question, and at the same time think about worrying that you may not have the answer. You end up identifying with what you're thinking about. And you create the will to fail for this reason: your mind was occupied by the thought of failure, instead of being occupied by the search for the exam answer and response. You cannot think of two thoughts at once.

A negative thought and a positive thought cannot co-exist in your present consciousness. Your mind can only play with one thought at a time. It is why Buddhists repeat endlessly a particular mantra. It is not about the mantra. It is about emptying their minds - peace of mind by blocking intrusions.

Don't confuse this mental stance, with all the musings about positive thinking. This is not an effort in positive thinking. This is about taking a new and radical observer relationship with your mind. If you don't create this observer relationship you end up in the default position of identifying yourself with what your mind happens to put in your consciousness.

So when an unwanted memory is tossed up by your fitful oceanic mind, for your conscious embrace, do not try just to discard it. Immediately direct your mind to think specifically of something else. And do it immediately. The only way to stop an unwanted thought is to replace it - consciously and deliberately. You can only have one thought at a time in any one moment.

Get used to the idea of being an observer to your mind and from that standpoint managing your mind. Everyone's mind left alone is unruly. Your mind will always require your leadership. Left on its own, you are in trouble.

This becomes particularly true as you go along in life, and accumulate so many experiences that can be easily triggered. And your need to be selective, increases.

Most people are not used to boldly telling their minds what to think. But sooner or later you will have to learn to manage your mind like you manage your body. You have to become an observer to your mind, just like you are an observer to your body.

When your mind has an unwanted thought, most people will say, well, that is what I am thinking about. But that is not the exact truth. An unwanted thought pops up spurred by an associative subconscious. You did not choose it. You do not choose the itch that surfaces on your body. So you should not be saying that this unwanted thought is what I am wanting to think. It becomes so, only if you let it remain, and engage it.

You have to keep telling yourself to remain on the shore in a constant observer position in dealing with the sea of your mind. Sitting on its shore you will be astonished in wonder at the tumultuous ocean that your mind can be.

The whole idea of your becoming years is to get your consciousness to engage in self-direction.

You want your life to be a refection of your own self directed efforts in understanding what is true and therefore real.

Putting your self directing energies to what your mind chooses for thoughts, is a key to taking charge of your life. Little kids let their minds be shoved around by whatever emotions are hanging out in their heads. You have been there - done that.

Growing up is stopping this. Grown up means taking charge of what your mind is about to wallow in, and choosing to think only chosen thoughts - loyal to the truth you understand, and have made your own.

Your mind is for chosen thoughts.

If it is being used by unchosen ideas, your mind is a running engine just burning gas - going nowhere you have chosen.

But the consequences are more than just having a mind running around like a car without a driver.

What we think, we become.

What you allow yourself to think, you become.
What you direct your mind to think, you become.

You want to live your life on thoughts you choose - to become what you choose.

This is the self direction you must achieve in your energetic becoming years

Chapter 13

The Engineering of Luck

Straight and to the point: the luck of life is the people you meet. It comes from the individuals that somehow meet you.

To increase the possibility of good things happening to you, what can you do?

Simple: meet more people, and create more relationships when ever and where ever you can.

It is especially important to start between the ages of 18 and 28, the beginning time of your becoming, when you are freshly grown up, and opening yourself up to the next phase of your life. You are suddenly free to delve into the forest of differing individuals in a world apart from your growing-up relationships. With the end of your childhood status, you gain full time liberty to involve yourself with any one of the unique persons alive with you on the planet - currently some six to seven thousand million individuals. You could not ask for more choice.

Except for windfalls of winning lotteries and finding oil in your back yard, absolutely everything good that comes to you, will involve a relationship with another person that helped make it happen.

You just have to stand still, and reflect a moment to convince yourself that this is, in fact, absolutely true.

So now: commonsense will suggest to you that the more people you meet, the more opportunities there will be for human beings to know you, to relate to you, and so to help you.

The truth is that most people do not make much of an effort to meet new people.

This is particularly true of young people between 18 and 28, even though this is a period of their highest energy, and for many not yet married, a time of their greatest personal freedom.

Young people are just not used to taking the initiative to meet unfamiliar persons. They never really had to do it. No need. Family and friends are all that was needed to go thru the period of physically growing. But on completing this phase, the idea of heading out to meet new people would be a new and strange effort for young persons. They are shy, because they don't really know what will happen if they deliberately made this effort.

But you, as someone going past 18 years of age, will just have to have a sit down with yourself, and lecture yourself, that going out to meet your fellow humans, has a purpose important to your life, and that you will just have to make the effort. It has consequences for which there is no substitute.

So when you see a person that you might like to know, you will actually stand up, smile and make it happen - somehow. That "somehow" is tricky, because in being aggressive, any awkward conduct can make you instantly unattractive. There are no rules for being intimate - for approaching people. Every moment has its own immediacy. With some common sense, just try.

It is more likely that your efforts to meet more people will come in your willingness to attend functions and occasions that bring people together. It is natural not to spend time going to gatherings that have no compelling personal interest. You might lower that bar, and force yourself out to more gatherings of possible interest, having in mind a deliberate purpose simply to get to meet and know more of your fellow humans.

But meeting new people is not meant to be a "hello" and goodbye". Meeting new people is   "hello and persisting" when a relationship may be attractive and possible - by whatever means the moment will allow.

Persistence leads to luck - almost always. This is an ancient rule that makes sense.

When you are persisting, you are compelling attention. And attention is what brings you opportunity with people. You stand out individually. By reason of your persistence you become known, and opportunity is engaged. Most often without some persistence, nothing happens. So you keep making contact as best you can without being obtrusive - meaning to create more occasions for meeting, and let them play out.

Don't be afraid to let yourself be forward with an honesty that speaks of your being open and genuine - more easily believable in younger people than in older persons.

To a normal good hearted young person, this thought of going to meet people and relate to them for the possible advantage it might bring, is not a simple matter. This will just not feel right.

Should you want to meet and relate to people just to seek your own advantage? Are you going to genuinely face another person to just fish ingenuously for opportunities that a personal relationship might provide? Hoping you might get lucky with a relationship that brings you good fortune?

Is this motive for meeting another person not predatory? Crass. Zero class. Can you treat your fellow human persons who are canoeing with you in the same river of time, just as tools for your own use? Are the people around you simply an orchard of trees from which you pluck fruit? This is innately abhorrent. It should be so to anyone, but particularly to a young person starting off in life wishing everyone well.

Human beings hugely resent people trying to relate to them as tools for their use. Dogs will relate to humans to acquire food, protection, and affection. A human person accepts this from his puppy. It is only a dog. Nothing more is expected.

But with a human person meeting another human person, this is different. There is no meeting without some relating. Humans meeting are like passing stars getting into each others' ever present gravitational field. This is the touching of two nuclear fires that will feed on each other in expectation.

There is huge expectation at play underfoot, where in basic unspoken terms, there is an underlying force at work, in every person, effectively saying you will honor my existence with your free will and you will not be allowed to use my existence merely to honor your existence, and its needs.

So here then is the dilemma: you want to meet people to gain from them an advantage you desire. But persons you meet just for this purpose, once perceived, will react in repulsion.

It is also unrealistic, to say to yourself: "Ok, I am not going to make any effort to meet a person for my own advantage. It's a gross way of being. I am not going to be like that. It is wrong."

But you need relationships with people to survive and prosper. You really do. You are hurting yourself if you think you should not push forward to meet people, for your advantage. So how do you solve this?

There is only one real way for an honest person to handle any dilemma. Sit back and ask yourself a stark and simple question: "Well, what is the truth here? " Do what the French call a "tour d'horizon", a tour of the horizon. Look in every direction and state to yourself the truth you see.

As you look around, you will see that at least three things are true. One, you do need to use people to accomplish your career and economic goals. Two, it is wrong to approach people only to use them just for your own advancement and well being. Three, you know that people from whom you would take your own advantage, also would like to have their own human needs also satisfied in basic gratitude and loyalty.

So you know that what you may take or be given, should be returned in gratitude and loyalty. And if you agree with this unspoken obligation, then this is how you would approach gaining an advantage from a relationship.

With this understanding in place, you can in good conscience go about the human universe of persons, and meet as many individuals as you can, to help you journey to your dreams. But you know you must never be a taker, without being a giver.

A note must be added here:

This is the story of luck and how luck happens. It is put on the table here for you to consider because it is true, and because such thoughts flicker through the minds of almost all of us as young start-up adults. So at some point, this is something that all of us should also think through.

This will bring conflicting concerns to many thoughtful persons. When you start analyzing luck to see how you can create more luck for yourself, you are on the road to taking the luck out of luck, and are simply describing a task to be undertaken. The result, plainly spoken, makes you appear to be gaming people.

This is not to the taste of thoughtful young persons of goodwill, whose instincts are that people should be related to, for their own sake - meaning for the worthiness we see in them as persons riding their lives with us in our time.

Such individuals think relationships should always be for this higher purpose of mutual desire for each other's being, and well being.

This seeking out and approaching people for what they can do for us, albeit an intelligent and practical effort, can also be seen as demeaning to young spirits tuned in to this higher purpose. They will not be comfortable with thoughts of consciously using people.

A young person of goodwill can easily understand the intelligence of this effort to meet people in seeking opportunity. But they will be troubled by it. There is no easy answer.

Instead of being paralyzed in hesitancy, It is always best to get up close to see if a real relationship is possible, and let ensuing events guide you. When you have these discomforting concerns, don't decide until you see the real picture in detail, instead of just in theory.

It could be your luck to have your opportunity and your concerns be both well met.

Chapter 14

Encountering Genetics

Be Aware - Go easy

This is all about a moment. The moment you first experience a startling difference in another human being. The moment when you see facial features you are not used to looking at; hear language and words, that are not yours; confront a different skin tone, or see an appearance you cannot explain.

The associations that fill our minds when we encounter what's familiar, are not there. This instant vacuum makes us wonder what to think. And we got to think. Because this unfamiliarity is not about some new, colorful bird in your back yard, but about a fully alive human being, like ourselves.

Strangeness is seldom attractive. What we know, is what we relate to.

Yet in front of you is another human being; this is a human person that came to be, just like you did, encountering the same chance at genetics that form and detail our own physical bodies - and can as well direct the performance of our personality.

And how did we acquire our bodies? Well, with very little effort. In fact with absolutely no effort on our part. We had no say as to our being a guy or a girl. What our facial features are like. Big chin, little chin. Little nose, big nose. Eyes slanting or round. Square head or narrow head. We were genetically assigned a hair color, a eye color, a skin color and complexion.

So if people find you handsome, or beautiful to look at, and have a natural smile, it is not your fault. It's not your doing. It is something done to you. It is all based on the genetics given to you, assigned to you before you ever saw the light of your first day.

So if people say you are beautiful, you have to say to yourself: "Well, not exactly my own doing. What I am in terms of what I was able to choose, is another story." Still folks easily go from how you look as an individual, to how you are as a person.

When people praise how you look, you probably don't correct them. But in your heart you know the real story. You accept the praise without a word.

So when you first meet and look at someone you find distastefully different, you got to remember what the real story is for you, and that this is also the real story for the person in front of you. His or her's appearance to you is a no-choice deal for him or her. And you have to understand that they would also be very aware of the likelihood of dislike against them when they are living surrounded in a different society.

So again, this is an important part of what you already know about people you have never met:
That when you do meet them, you are confronting a person who is immersed in physical looks that he did not chose, and who expresses a personality that may be driven by inclinations which he also never chose.

To put this in stark language, we can say that we physically present ourselves to other people appearing almost as a doll that someone else made for us, that the person within did not chose. This unchosen appearance is what people first see.

It is only by looking beyond this appearance that people can define by experience with us, our unique individuality - seeing what we have chosen to do with what has physically been given and imposed on each of us in birth.

Somewhere in all this, there will be both a comforting and discomforting fact for everyone. But the point of discussing it, is this:

That in being honest about each other's reality, let this awareness temper our distaste and our compulsion to dismiss different looking people and difficult to deal with personalities. This could have been your own person in that genetic driven body and personality. Nothing we know, can foreclose that possibility.

These realities can be encountered in unexpected moments. One such memorable moment, occurred in Jamaica while teaching a business ethics course in a university's MBA program (Master degree in Business Administration). There were some 28 students in the room, all were Jamaicans of African heritage, from 22 years of age to 30. All were college graduates.

We were discussing the need to focus on understanding the individual dimension before assessing blame in disputes. We discussed, as we have here in a previous chapter, that persons are born, with no opportunities to chose what kind of body they must live with, or the people to whom they will belong, or where they first will encounter life, and how we all are subject to dealing with what is abruptly handed to us at birth.

This was an unusual discussion, as these considerations are seldom openly discussed.

But in the moment after expressing this to the class, the instant reaction was surprising. Movement stopped. They sort of shied away from looking at the front of the room where I was sitting. There was a sudden solemn concern on their faces. I looked behind me to see what was causing this reaction. There was nothing but the blackboard. Then a girl at the back of the classroom quietly said in a low voice: "So, it is not our fault."

It was a young woman who said this. But in the moment, I saw it coming from a young kid, a 10 year old, who had encountered people not happily relating to her, and worried then why there were people she didn't even know who disapproved of her, and wondered what she might have done that couldn't be understood - learning later of the extensive prejudice towards different skin color and culture.   Here, belatedly, in clear focus was a kid's reassuring moment. "So, it's not our fault."

Considering the options we do not have in choice of body, genetics, and birth place, it is not easy to be a human being and having to bridge the genetic differences bestowed on us as individual persons. So few of us have the willingness to recognize how arbitrarily these differences come about.

An honest effort begins in a good humored acceptance that our physical differences and personality differences, and the consequent cultural differences, are all not to due to any individuals' personal choice. These are imposed differences given to each person at birth. Compared to the gift of life itself which we all share, these difference are pocket change in respecting each other.

So let's be easy and gentle as we approach each other, and give a realistic acknowledgment as to how all this is physically imposed on each of us as individual humans.

You will travel beyond your own personal region of growing up, and become confronted with the stark differences in humans not part of your growing-up world. Maintaining a clear consciousness that people do not individually create and cause the basic physical and cultural differences you see in them, will take your constant attention.

How you begin to handle this now, will probably be how you will deal with it through the rest of your life.

You will need an attitude of honesty about each other, and a personal willingness to see yourself in other people's shoes.

Chapter 15

Confronting the Rocks of Genetics - in Personalities

This is a pocket idea. A note to yourself, to fold and keep in your pocket, as you trudge thru life, tangling and untangling yourself, stepping through this planet's forest of personalities.

This note is about limits on what you can do - when you come upon people that stand in your presence, confront your needs and desires, and become directly obstructing obstacles to a happy existence.

Should you make an effort to change them? How much can you really change them?

Well, firstly, you have to know what you are dealing with, in trying to change a person's attitudes, that you cannot and will not accept.

The optimism and energy of youth, will not want to hear this. But when you are looking to dig up and change deep seated behavior, you are more likely to be unearthing hard rocks that won't break, rather than clay you can mold.

In clear words, don't be optimistic about changing entrenched behavior. It will be long, arduous work, with a highly uncertain outcome.

As short as fifty years ago, there was more favorable thinking. It was thought and widely taught, that people and their personalities could be readily changed. The perspective then was that to effect change, just put your arms around the offending person, and with boundless attention and affection you could "nurture" a person to abandon unwanted behavior, in the young or old. It was believed that most conduct was subject to change if enough nurturing was invested in the offending person.

This view has now been largely abandoned. A new reality has been studied and recognized. You would find its best summary in a book of essays entitled Why the Reckless Survive, by Melvin Konner, (Viking Penguin, 1990, p. 223)

This new research and thinking can be quickly stated: that the study of actual evidence shows that the personality (the tendencies) of an individual human being is predominantly (say 60%) genetically based and derived. Included would also be the cultural characteristics common to a recognized group of humans.The other 40% or so is a product of an experienced environment, and still remains subject to the nurturing efforts of others.

The conclusion is that the core of what you are dealing with in a human's personality, can be the same confrontation with genetics inherited with the body at birth. Just as in a person's bodily appearance, the content of both body and personal genetics are no one's self choice.

This consciousness should be an awareness, that compels us to a kinder, more tolerant approach to each other - an approach of becalming realism. When you need to drill down to deeply understand an individual person that interests you, this understanding should be in the forefront of your thoughts.

Someday you are going to be relating to a person who may become deeply involved in your living. There will be trouble. You may be faced with a conclusion, that the incompatibility is genetic sourced, and you will have to make the hard decision that there is no remedy.

And you will have to disengage and walk away, understanding that you have encountered a clear reality of genetics which you cannot change. A hard choice to make, but it is eased in understanding that you are bowing to a reality not of your own making.

Inevitably - a time will come. There will be a moment when you will find yourself digging for this brief note.

You never know when you will have to pull it from your pocket.

Chapter 16

On Loving What You Got

But what if you don't

Do you remember reading this in a previous chapter :

Look at yourself. Not too long ago, you first saw light.
You were then introduced to a nice person, who said
she was your mother. Then there should have been
someone right after that, who said he was your
father.

You had nothing to do with choosing these people. It
was done for you.

You had nothing to do with choosing the place on
this planet where all this happened; but you are stuck
with the locale of where it did. You did not choose it.
The time, the year, the month, the day when you
began, was imposed on you.

So here you are, living with people you didn't choose, and you have been put in a place on this planet that you also did not choose. No consultation about the timing.

Worse. You were given a body off the rack. No chance to choose skin color, curly hair or not, tall or short? No choice. Sex? What you see is what you got. No consultation. None.

How fair is this! Everyone is equally treated this abruptly, and then bulldozed over the edge of nothingness into life.

What can you say? Well say truthfully what you do know: that we all wake up to the reality of living in the same boat - called "Zero Choice".

Anyone of us could have had what befell to some other person. Think about it. The entire body platform and social platform on which your person begins to exist, is something upon which you were plopped - just dropped. So for what you got, you cannot be blamed. Nor can you be praised for what you were born with, as your own achievement.

Well, you read this, and you may still be very annoyed at what you see in the mirror - morning, noon and night. When you are at the age of 18 thru your early 20's, you are surrounded by everyone else's energy in trying to have a more desirable appearance - physical and social. If you are honest, you are likely to see yourself using your energy doing the same.

And if you do not look at your appearance with super pride, you are likely to look at yourself with super depression. And no one is about to talk you out of your depression. You are not happy. You can do nothing about it. So what is the point of further discussion?

The points are many. You know you will be living a long time. So take a moment and visit yourself down line - ten years from now. You still will be looking the way you are with no really major change in the mirror.

But in your mind, there will be a change. You will not care as much. You will be more used to seeing yourself grown up. You won't have as much time or interest to worry about your comparative good looks. Time has gone on, and your lack of a super appearance (if you had such a thought) has not hurt you. You will be more calmed down about not having received the body you would have liked.

Between 18 and 28, you will have seen people who do not have super appearances, but nevertheless have super careers. You will know then that dazzling good looks is not necessary for a great life. By then you will have seen enough beautiful people who are absolute airheads - offering nothing but their born-with gifts, and nothing of earned merit. By then you will know physically unpretentious people, who are well loved and respected as great personalities. So you will be calmed down about the urgency of having a great appearance.

At this point you will be ready for some different thinking.

Here is what should slowly be coming to mind: With the passage of time you will be willing to look at the big picture, Then you can allow yourself just to be impressed by the gift of life itself. You have a self, that is alive and unique to all creation - and this is yours. And when you really see this, your attitude is simply that it is great to be alive - everything else is pocket change.

Whatever else may happen, or not happen, will not sink your boat, or your willingness to always sail on.

The point of being a great personality should have your attention. Because this happens regardless of physical attractiveness and any social status. Somehow we know this. But what is it about a great personality that is so great and elevating and causes people to lean towards them and seek to be with them? We call it charisma. This means what?

It is simple - almost too simple. This great personality means that a person is able to show that when he faces people, that he personally likes them, that he is glad they exist, that he is able to know them.

A great personality is able to communicate this by physical demeanor and words that are voiced, that come from being simply genuine.

Meeting such a personality is an experience. It is being confronted by someone with a wide open door through which you see yourself being freely and enthusiastically and personally liked. A great personality makes everyone almost instantly feel good - showing everyone that he or she is personally desired. A person just offering born-with good looks, could never achieve this.

The reason for discussing this is to make the point that making yourself desirable does not require the gifts of birth - good looks, telegenic smile, and a social standing. By genuinely putting your arms around everyone your heart can hold, you can make yourself into a great personality - to be more desired than such gifts of birth could ever achieve for you.

But such a person not only embraces other people, they also happily embrace themselves. They refuse to dislike what they have been given in life. They stand with it and live contentedly.

A great people-affirming personality has no hidden agenda of hating and being resentful of what they were given at birth. If they did, it could not be hidden. People will always sense any ill feeling you may have about your self, and would by led to confirm your own self-disdain. This you do not want.

There is something else you do not want. You do not want to have any other life than your own.

In the climb for fortune and fame -which ultimately means the drive to be desired by those with whom you live - you will see others come easily to great advantage, by good luck, by just being in the right place at the right time, by knowing the right people, by having the right talents at the right moment. You will often see your own situation not being so favored in spite of your own honest efforts. Unfairness comes to mind and you can easily arrive at an annoyed state, generally called envy.

The problem with envy is that it is such an angry emotion that it obscures the facts you need to know to be envious. You never really know what is behind the tale off some one else's good fortune. You never really know the actual conditions or limitations of time or extent in its excited disclosure. Such information is naturally self sealed. So you can never really know how great should be your envy. If you knew all there is to know, you may not want to be so envious. But in most cases you just do not know.

So you should spare yourself the trouble of allowing envy to displace your own energy going forward. You want your own luck for your own life, not anybody else's.

One of the unspoken instigators of envy, is the notion that there is somehow a limited supply of good luck in the world that allows good fortune to befall you. Hence, your anxiety is aroused when someone else becomes suddenly a joyous recipient of unearned unexpected good fortune. You become somewhat depressed as if you are seeing your own chances diminish and your hopes for your own future dimmed.

Part of the painful experience of dwelling with envy is bringing this dark roof of worry over your head.

But there is no rationale for this. It is just like that ready belief that if the rich get richer, the poor must become poorer because there is a limited supply of money in the world. This is one of these unspoken assumptions that persists because people seldom pause to think such things through. It does not work like that. Similarly, there is no limited supply of the possibilities of good fortune happening to you.

The first murder recorded in the world's literature, was the killing of Adam and Eve's son Abel by his brother Cain. The Biblical Book of Genesis describes the motive as Cain's envy that his brother Abel's offering was more pleasing to God than his own. And he killed him for this reason. The reason was an assumption that God in being pleased with Abel's offering, could, therefore, have no additional willingness to favor Cain. The Bible goes on to detail the fury of God over this mistaken assumption and its unwarranted response by Cain.

This is an important lesson in the world of envy thinking. What is given to someone else does not diminish the good fortune that can be given to you.

Everyone has their own deal in living their life. You want your own deal. Not anyone else's. With pride in your own unique life, let your own life happen to you. It diminishes you to want anyone else's.

Bottom line to all this:

Be happy about yourself, and people will follow in kind.

Chapter 17

Joining the Traffic of Impersonal Humanity on the Move

Leaving the road of growing up and heading
down the ramp
to the fast lane highways in an impersonal
world

It is a here-I-go moment. You sort of never forget it. You are around 18 years old. High school is done. You got plans. And you go for it. Most of the time It means moving out of your family house. Time for you to be you. To be on your own.

In most families, it happens on a certain day, without a lot being said out loud. You're joining the military service. Heading off to college. Or getting a job, and soon moving to live with friends.

However it happens, you end up on a ramp, cruising down to join the rushing traffic on the highways of the impersonal world - already long in progress without you, racing along without ever needing you. People oblivious of you, will hardly pause to note your joining them. But they will soon learn what is in store for them - and that is you.

But on the brink of doing this, you, yourself, should pause, and take stock of these people already on the road.

They all carry around an awareness about a set of continuing concerns that commonly intrude on their lives - formed thru years of encountering them. Their awareness varies, but the topics of their concerns are the same, and await your joining them with your own take on everyday encounters.

Such common concerns that will confront you are: dealing with government; the always possible entanglement with law courts; what you should think about democracy; why should you be expected to believe in new science based stuff; who to trust; what personal reputation should you carefully guard.

With everybody else you will come to wonder: how do I personally avoid being dubiously displayed on the Internet; how do I know when not to rely on people; and wonder when I might need a mentor; how do I know when people are professional in what they do; and how do I know who are the dependably intelligent people around me.

As a member of the world's first generations to have grown up covered in the hot house of high tech media, you will want to have available your own critical thinking of what is happening to you in this radically new all day 24/7 media immersion. It has never before been experienced by the generations of humanity preceding you.

The quicker you get on board with the going concerns of the people tearing around this "new to you" impersonal world, the quicker you will get yourself untied and unconfined to a kid's narrow world of thought.

Sooner or later, these subjects of going concern are forced on everyone. It happens in their confrontation with the sheer force of human activity - everywhere around them. So you will have these same encounters. You will become part of a world sharing these concerns, sharing the same awareness, and sharing the need for answers.

Inevitably, you will join these conversations. You will be facing these same forces of life that create these concerns in the current traffic of humans - on the impersonal highway you're joining after 18.

Whether you like it or not, you should have views on all these topics that will, and often abruptly, command your attention one day.

So here is a chance for you to pause and exam ahead these every day concerns that will be coming your way. You do not want to be forced to deal with them on the fly. You need your own thought-out views. You do not want to be pushed to adopt the thoughts of other people simply because you have not paused to think for yourself.

You need your own thinking.

Many of the chapters to follow, will ask you to pause and check out your thinking on various topics which are like boulders we all climb over and around in everyday life, and for which you will want to have some prepared thinking - that comes from your own self-directed thinking.

The boulders of reality we all must climb over, are never handled well with instant thoughts. You do not want people to experience you as a kid caught easily in never having had a thought about the "why" of the difficult stuff that surrounds and controls life for all of us.

You will want people to experience you as a savvy young person who is really aware and thoughtful. Somebody to be dealt with. Some one to be listened to. Because you do have something to say. People will want to experience you as a new self directed thinker, a self directed person.

This can only happen if you have given thought to basic things already on people's minds. We will do this in the chapters that follow.

Chapter 18

The Pixel People in Your Life

Taking the Shine off your Humanity

Chances are this is really true: Think of the total time in your 21st century life, you have spent on this planet looking at a human face.

Chances are that half of this time was not spent looking at a real live human face, eyes to eyes.

Instead, it was spent looking at pixels electrically actuated to resemble a real human face - displayed in a rectangle box presenting people to you in movies, cartoons, live TV of instant news and entertainment. The color, the movement, the simultaneous sounds are life-like. The box puts out the entire range of sensory input of sound and sight that represents a life-like human person. Your eyes are captured by the box like a magnet seeking a refrigerator door.

This could easily have been how you have spent the most hours in your life in facing a human face. This means possibly that you have spent more hours since you have been three years old looking at a pixel face, than a real human face.

If this were true, then most of your life time spent visually engaged with a human face, was not spent in mutual awareness. This would be an astonishing situation.

Your face to face experience has actually been just with a box displaying a pixelated face created by points of light.

So what? What can be the harm?   The damage is actually this: Occupying your mind with pixelated people can dehumanize you. How so?

The harm is your getting accustomed to shutting down your normal personal response of dealing with mutual awareness, when later visually engaging an actual human life. Since the beginning of human existence, being engaged with a human face, meant a mutual awareness of each other.

Now, however, with the invention of electrically excited pixel lights vividly presenting live appearing people to your senses, these apparently alive faces of humans engage you - when actually no one is there in front of you.

This pixel displayed person disrupts your own and everyone's normal way of experiencing another person in front of you. It disrupts mutual awareness that is expected. It blanks out the self consciousness of your mind from being aware of a real person living and breathing and acting in free will, that you normally expect to be right in front of you, but is not.

But the harm can only happen in one way: The harm comes when this massively happens, and it is massively happening when millions and millions of people spend more than three hours every day facing people on media devices.

This particularly effects young and developing individuals. It cuts off and replaces their opportunity to grasp and learn the unspoken realities of the human person - that only mutual awareness, sheer presence and at hand intimacy can provide.

The harm is that it dulls a person's capacity for perception, as he gets accustomed to dealing with people without feeling their personal presence.

You were not born for this. The point of living is your relationships with other persons.

But when pixel people populate your life, the consequence is this: a person's empathy for his fellow humans is atrophied - meaning cut short of where it normally would be, and no further growth easily happens.

A person's sensitivity to the consciousness of his fellow humans, and their feelings and needs, are dulled by hours and hours spent with pixel faces, without undergoing any relationship with them. And then when you are face to face with actual people, you react by induced habit with no expectation of personal awareness, carrying over the same limited spectator-like disengagement you have with the pixel people you spend so much time with - on the box.

Your real life engagement with human faces becomes anesthetized - meaning you do not realize you have lost the wakefulness of awareness - just like what happens to you in the hospital when being prepared for surgery. Your personal awareness is cut off.

The result of too much pixel face time is that your natural awareness of another person's state of mind and heart has been trained out of you in varying degrees when you do face real people. The end result is that a person becomes accustomed to being less aware of the feelings of people around them.

This is particularly hurtful to young people as they confront new people in an impersonal world, where they most need to be alive in awareness, and quick to understand and react to the new individuals they meet.

When you observe and learn about people thru the media box, your instincts are to react like they are real persons but your outreach hits a wall. You half realize this, but pay little attention to your disability to relate to pixel people.

When your life's experiences with human individuals become in large part a result of pixel viewing, you are not getting a real life understanding of what there is to understand about an individual person. You cannot get the feel of what's going on with such an individual. Where his head is at. You are losing that prized ability of all really successful CEO's, leaders of people, which is to have such detailed understanding about the individual persons he is dealing with and depending on. An end result is that - being dulled - you lose good judgment about people.

So the most damaging consequence of your personal powers being daily absorbed in a television or computer monitor's pixellated representation of other human beings, is your getting used to - accustomed to - observing people without the possibility of mutual awareness.

Again, what is the problem with this? It's a killer of empathy. You are being accustomed to seeing people as objects to be dealt with, instead of as a human being whom you can sense is looking to know you, and possibly with whom you may have a relationship. You accept that there is no possibility of a relationship with a pixel face.

If your experience in looking at a human face has mostly been thru pixels, you acquire an ability never previously experienced in humans dealing with each other. This the ability to dismiss the presence of a real human being just like you dismiss a pixel person - without a blink as you touch the off button.

With your sensibilities of expecting mutual awareness being dulled, you get into the easy habit of turning off real people, just like you turn off pixel people. You do it without another thought.

You don't say 'goodbye' when you turn off the television box or any media device.

And so you gradually can learn to turn away from real life people, just like you turn off the pixel box. No mutual awareness. No engagement with another human's awareness. No relationship expected.

Your normally expected awareness and empathy with live human persons in your life, just gets habitually ignored. Your understanding of the people around you is diminished and dumbed down. The way people have usually experienced each other for thousands of years, is suddenly slowed, cut off and changed by the rising flood of daily focusing on pixel people. The experience has consequences

There is no understanding possible of another human being without a capacity for empathy with that person. If you become incapable of empathy for other people, you are a disaster as a human being.

If you let this continue without thoughtful restriction, you will be in trouble everywhere you go on this planet, except an empty desert.

So what are we saying here? You are born into a world that is just now universally experiencing pixelated people - now being the last 30 years. No civilization before your time has had any experience with this new reality of people spending massive amount of time with pixel representations of other humans instead of with each other.

No generation has yet had time to understand the consequence of this new immersion of electronic based human relationships, and draw lessons for themselves and to pass onto those following them. We know there is a coming consequence. We still don't know the extent of the damage that this alteration of natural perception is doing to a human's grasp of awareness of each other. Human experience has never before encountered this.

This is not a normal happening by any standards of human history. There is something different here. This is an experience of humans being absorbed by their pixelated representations without mutual awareness. The experience is not just that this is happening, but the extent of it's happening. Its imposition during the people's daily duration of being awake is huge and increasing.

A once in a while happening creates little effect in a human's experience. But when it absorbs two to three hours of each and everyday life of hundreds of millions of individual people, then we are having a massive experience. It's something else.

Degrees of things, change into different kind of things. This is the QTQ Principle. Quantity transforms quality - meaning the nature of things and their effects get altered as their quantity is greatly changed.

In giving all this a think and a wonder, you want to ask: How do you handle this?

First, make yourself acknowledge exactly what is occurring to your own consciousness when you passively watch pixelated persons - reflecting how limited is this experience.

The experience of seeing and interacting with people thru pixels and processed sound gives a false sense of disclosing reality.

Companies with offices all over the globe often meet and know each other just thru Internet enabled video conferencing. But at some point there will be a conference held in a hotel where they actually meet in physical presence. Then the ensuing conversations are predictable. There is never ending joking - sort of - where people say, "I thought I knew you, but you are nothing like I imagined from seeing you on the monitor."

In other words, don't get too comfortable with what you see and judge from video time. Pixels cannot communicate the personal aura of what you need to know.

We all must come to judgments about people we deal with. Usable judgments about people require the kind of mutual awareness that comes only from being in their presence. Because this is a presence of a free will in motion - the essence of what we are dealing with.

You just have to teach yourself to hold back your opinions and personal decisions until you actually meet.

All of this is something for you to ponder: this Godzilla capacity of technical communication to absorb and jail our senses. It easily grabs and steals from us our real moments of now, - which is our living time to engage the personal presence of real persons. This is the only basis for the trusting relationships we want and need.

We've got problems here, the reach of which we have yet to understand. In your lifetime you should expect to be part of a controlling effort.

This massive technology embracing our physical senses, is broadening its absorption of all human communication, and it is doing this slowly and forcibly like a rising tide. There is a horizon-to horizon stealth, that escapes our critical notice.

Speculating on massive changes in human life noted in ancient lore, we can easily imagine that no one thought at the beginning of Noah's Great Flood that it would ever seriously amount to anything of great consequence. Really serious beginnings hide their nature.

You don't see changes when you are swimming in a rising tide. Think about where you are - your own situational awareness in the midst of all this.

It will be a challenge for your lifetime.

Chapter 19

Details are Fuel for Glory

In The Engine Room of Decisions - Your New Attitude

Sometime after becoming 18, you will be part of this:

In the impersonal (non family world) people who do not know each other very well, get together to make decisions about a project, a business, an enterprise. There will be meetings and discussions around a lunch table, in a school on big projects, or in a company launched forum.

When you are included in such meetings as a young person, most often you will be a rookie. Not much of a contribution will be expected of you. But you can change this expectation, and you should.

Bearing in mind that you never get "a second chance to make a first impression", there is only one way to go. Whatever subject the meeting is going to undertake, you will sit down beforehand and think through all the details about any of the subjects that could possibly come up in the meeting you will be attending.

Then list all possible questions that may be asked in the meeting about these details. Look for answers in an Internet search engine: their history, their currency, examples of their use, every point of relevant curiosity that you can imagine that might be asked. Make a few phone calls around the world to verify what you know will be brought up, so you are likely to have the most current information than anyone else. Then consider the differing viewpoints that can arise over the same set of facts. Make an evaluation in your own mind of the merits of alternative thinking.

You will be making an effort that others are not likely to do - to spend the time to master the issues, as you are doing in this preparation. Always make yourself more prepared than anyone else.

Armed with this, you go to the meeting, and as you get near the subject of these details that you have researched, you make a point to respectfully interject and add your information. Chances are that your efforts have outgunned even more senior people.

Because what you have done is brought to this meeting the edge of your youthful energy to run this extra mile to have all relevant factual details at hand. This gives rise to immediate appreciation of, shall we say, your helpful existence. You want to be known as that person that can be relied upon, to go this extra mile.

In a class at a graduate business school, on one occasion, I gave my students tee shirts to wear that said in bold print: "He who has the most facts, Wins!" (This is true, if you also add that you can never escape the need to have predictive intelligence for good judgment.) The tee shirts announce that you have the ambition to "master" the details of whatever you are involved in.

It means that you have said to yourself that you will never go to a meeting that is part of a decision effort, unless you are prepared to bracket every area of possible interest with your up to the minute information.

Now this is work. But it is work that that will put your own worth on display. And it will be remembered. And it will encourage reliance on you. And reliance on you will cause your growing inclusion in the enterprise.

Later in class, after discussing the tee shirt as the second cardinal rule for engaging in meetings, we addressed the first, the premier rule preparing for decision meetings. This is simply and absolutely stated: Never step into such a meeting, without first having a private meeting with your self to figure out how you want it to end.

Information without direction, is pointless.

This means that you have figured out in advance what's going to be said, and you have figured out in advance what decisions should be made. Only then, do you go to engage.

So all of this is to say that as a young person, when you are included in a meeting, don't just go there, only to sit like a pelican on a dock post. Your presence is never to be taken lightly. Make yourself someone that knows and can be relied upon to know. And when others in your new impersonal world, have that kind of experience with you, they will be coming back to you.

Not a lot of us understand that the intelligence which senior people are looking for in meetings (and elsewhere), is predictive awareness. This is based on an ability to acquire, and be aware of, the details that make things and people actually work, or not work. This detail-oriented intelligent person should be you.

What does a detail-oriented person do? You look at every known item that is a necessary part of a project, and ask yourself: what has to be for this necessary detail to exist. Then you take the answer to this question and drill down on it with this same question: what now has to be for this newly found underlying detail to exist. This is drilling down on details. This is what mastering details means. Drilling down.

BOTTOM LINE: Mastering Details is what the Master's Touch is all about on this planet. This is true in Art, and in War and in every human operation. It has been the secret of individual excellence in every century.

If you are unwilling to drill down on details, consider yourself as unwilling to be the Master In what you are involved.

It has been the age old problem, that when people are young they have the energy required for this intelligence and excellence. But when older, lack of energy often inhibits the effort to go after details unless you acquired this determination when younger.

But when younger, it is the time of life when persons have the least tolerance for working details that could be boring. So detail work is most often just avoided by younger people. There is your opportunity to be outstanding: Unusual excellence in work when you are young, means a willingness to throw your energy into boring activity. This is the state of play you are in. You make a decision which way you want to go. You are going to be the highly prized young person who is willing to master details, or you are not.

The young bright willing spirits that can overcome this detail phobia at an early age, will be the winners.

So the counsel here is to get over the idea that boring work on details is not worth your time,

The winning often results in more than you imagined. You will come to see that the first person to master details on any project, and communicates this, that person will ultimately become part of controlling it, even, if being young, he or she is not formally in charge.

In college I had a roommate from Madras, India. On ending any project, he indulged in this final victory flourish as his own dramatic, narcissistic routine: He would stand on his desk chair, and hold his open hand at eye level, and announce loudly for the millionth time: "My Dad told me to put the world in my hand, like an orange, and...(pausing for effect) PEEL it - bit by bit." Then the satisfied son would get down off his chair, his imagined orange having been peeled. Dumb routine. Smart idea.

It is only after getting out of school and confronting the hard realities of outcome oriented work, that most of us understand (if we ever do) about the way to "peel the orange" - is to drill down and experience every detail. No skin left on the orange.

So we become ahead of everybody else in drilling down and mastering the details of all that we touch with our minds. Details are the required pathways to mastering the substance of anything - always.

Chapter 20

Managing What People Expect from You

Creating the One Reputation You Really Want

Up to age 18, you are living in a world where everyone meaningful to you, knows you - personally. It's an easy life to deal with, a great life. But this ideal world stops for almost everyone quite abruptly.

Because after 18 you enter a world where the people you need and want, will probably not even know you. When you try to have a relationship with them, you can give them a resume describing yourself, but even after reading, it is never enough. They will be wanting to know more about you - as a person. And it's more than whether you speak well, dress decently, and are presumably honest.

Particularly because you are a young person, people will have a more pointed question about you.

Basically, it is this: people want to know if you are "reliable". Can you be trusted?

Young persons being 'unreliable' is their world wide default reputation. It is a legendary prejudice, with a lot of legends to back It up.

Pointless to say - just stating this world wide prejudice against young people of being unreliable persons, doesn't tell you much. It is some thing your Grandmother might mention with little consequence to your psyche.

But if you really paused to figure out that this prejudice is real, and how it could effect you, you would advance your concern for the world's perception of your reliability to Page One in your young life.

This means that you have a reputation for being unreliable before you have ever attempted anything anywhere. Just because you are new and young. How unfair is this?

You have to deal with this youth reputation for unreliability problem, and do it in two contexts. There is a beginning problem, and there is an everyday control problem.

As you start in the impersonal world, encountering people in your search for employment and responsibility, you should know that the older folks will meet your young self with this unflattering prejudice.

They will bring to any discussion with you, their experience of disappointments in dealing with young people not being reliable, not being dependable and not being focused.

Nothing may actually be said to you. But you should anticipate that a concern for your reliability will be their first filter in looking at you.

But in your being aware of it, you can help to diffuse it with with a deliberate act.

Here is the suggestion: In any formal or informal meeting with a prospective employer (or an older someone you are joining) you will come to an end of your discussion. At that point, you should take the initiative to sum up and state the future "action points" of what is understood that you will further do, or when you will further meet. Don't dwell on this recitation. Just be brief and decisive. Just say : "Ok, based on our discussion, this what I will be doing..."

You must be the one to do this, not the other guy in front of you. If he beats you to it, nevertheless repeat it back to him. It tells him that you are organizing in your mind a commitment to act, and that you are directing yourself to get it done. This sum-up style speaks reliability - without saying the word.

This is a simple thing to do. But when you are on the other side of the conversation, it's impressive. It separates you from the crowds of vague and "maybe" youths. You stand out as a young person who is in deliberate charge of his or her energy.

Even though it is critical for you to present yourself this way, in your beginning forays into employment in an impersonal world, it is also a productive way to end all your future meetings.

So you should be the one person at the end of your every meeting or interview to state a sum-up. This gives you the image of having a commanding clarity. It lets you take the mantle of leadership in an unobtrusive way.

But it is this commanding clarity that we now need to discuss. It is the foundation of an every day control of your reputation for reliability.

There is more to understand here. There is a particular point that needs your continuing awareness.

Whether you realize it or not, your everyday business (or operational) dealings with people are all played on a field called "promissory liability".

The two word label covers this idea, but let's spell it out concisely:

That if any words, you speak or write, could induce a reasonable person to rely on what is expressed to him, then you, wittingly or not, incur a promissory liability to perform.

If you are getting something in return, this could result in a court enforceable legal obligation to perform upon you.

But apart from this possibility of legal consequence, the concern here is for your every day casual business conversations. This is where there is a constant potential for unintended consequences that can really do damage to your personal reputation for reliability.

You write in an email or say in a phone conversation things like "we'll take care of this", or "let me look into this", or "I will see what I can do"' or "this sounds ok". Then you do nothing - no follow-on response.

These words and phrases casually said, nevertheless, may induce others to place actual reliance on you - that you will indeed make efforts to be helpful, and then get back to them. But in point of fact you end up doing absolutely nothing. After a few experiences like this with you, your personal reputation for reliability becomes an in house joke.

This is an everyday example of how loose language can get you into trouble. When you said these things, you probably had no specific intention to act. And perhaps you were just trying to avoid the confrontation of exposing your real thoughts. But by your polite words you induced a reliance that you would in fact do something. You did not hear yourself saying this specifically, but your listener did.

This is an every day example of how in talking around the edges, how in trying to be nice, or avoid taking a displeasing position, can unwittingly get you into trouble.

Watching your words that induce reliance on yourself in other people, has to be your new life long level of awareness. You must wear it like a wrist watch. You have to tell yourself that you have to work on being conscious of how other people hear you, or read your words.

You do this by developing the knack of placing yourself in other people's shoes, and then seeing yourself communicating to them.

With this habitual effort, you will have a constant check on yourself to ensure that you are not Inducing a reliance by what you are casually saying or writing - that on reflection, you really do not want to be there.

The key words here: Be sufficiently aware to <u>avoid inducing a reliance</u> on yourself that you do not intend.

You are not likely to be sued. But lacking an every day conscious control, it's a guaranteed consequence that your reputation for reliability will eventually dissolve into a mixture of a very disgusted disappointment and an amused disdain for your swift and easy words.

A straight forward way to avoid inadvertent reliance, is to make a point of telling people exactly what to rely and what not to rely in the sum-up of your conversation or email writing. Just say: " Here is what you can rely on ,,,,,,,"

Sum-ups are an important habit to acquire in dealing with people on projects. Taking charge at the end of any business conversation with your own stated sum-up, is the clearest indication to any one listening, that they are dealing with a first class person that will be dependable.

People will appreciate your candor and concern for clarity. Expectations are out in the open. It will also burnish your reputation for up front honesty.

The important consequence here is that you are actually managing the expectations of the people surrounding you. This is the key focus that enables you to be in charge of your life as you ride this planet with all kinds of uncontrollable fellow travelers.

Now this is going to be more difficult for you than it has been for all the civilizations that have preceded you.

You happen to have been born into life at a time when it is hugely difficult to be careful and thoughtful in your personal and business communications.

To be thoughtful and poised in what you are doing, now - in this life time of yours - takes significantly more effort and a more deliberate mindset.

For the first time in human living, people in present generations can be accosted into important conversations virtually 24 hours a day, on all seven days of the week without surcease. You are living in the new atmosphere of hi-tech casual hi-there communication.

Before your time, business communications were almost always conducted in protected environments of offices. Throughout the last century it was a deliberate art on where we placed telephones in our homes, and offices. People wanted separation and privacy - an atmosphere where one could deal thoughtfully with one's affairs.

Today's technology of cellphones, and iPads, email and texts, and instant messaging, makes each one of us instantly accessible 24 hours a day, regardless of whether we are in an office or in our bedroom, or otherwise occupied in private places.

Today, these safeguards for well considered business conversations are gone. Today our communications are spliced into the non-stop dervish dance of all that happens to us in any 24 hours of any day or night.

Being quickly eroded are the previous guarantees, that you will be accosted only in the customary times and places for business and planning discussions. Your surrounding environment was protected by an office setting, or a barrier to uncontrolled distractions.

But now you have to control your access to yourself with an aroused discipline. This is an effort that in earlier times you did not have to deal with.

This high tech 21st century that you were born to live in, is really harder to handle. We have brought upon ourselves intense difficulties of disruption and distraction that no human living before us, has ever had to deal with. Our communications are bound to be more loose, distracted and less sharp in thought.

Prior to only the last century, humans on this planet could only communicate afar with considerable care. It was a chore. Sharpen up the old quill, mix the ink to the right consistency, find some unused paper, etc. and then get a horse for delivery.

But then, in a quick succession of just recent decades, came telegraph, telephones, radio, and satellites, and finally arrived at IPhones and IPads - now worn with the intimacy of a T shirt. They stay with us wherever we happen to be worldwide.

Now, finally, we have arrived into a 24 hours a day exposure - no matter where our body happens to be - to the instant communications of emails, texts, and cell phones, and to the ultimate exposure of the instant intimacy of unexpected visual FaceTime calls.

Communication is no longer a controllable affair. It is a rapid free-fire deployment from any place where a body can be, at any time of day or night.

This means we are put in a position of being accosted by a demand for our considered communications in all kinds of unstable and distracting environments, where we can easily say things we have not sufficiently considered.

Bottom line:

Your reputation for being reliable, takes a more conscious effort now, than was necessary in the generations before you. You can be accosted more easily, and tripped up more easily in being seen to induce people 's reliance on you - because now you have so many more varied and compromising occasions to communicate.

So with this acute awareness, you must consciously create or consciously limit, what a reasonable person should understand in relying on your words, spoken, emailed or texted.

Put yourself in the place of the person listening to you. Hear yourself talking, and seek to understand what that listener would take away from hearing your words.

Put yourself in the place of the person reading your emails, texts, and letters. Before you send them, read them over envisioning the intended recipient reading exactly what is written, and be sensitive to what unintended reliance you may be inducing with your words.

Practice doing this. Practice speaking and writing using this reflecting lens to create a focus on the impact of your words. Be thoughtful in seeing how people are possibly being led to rely on you.

In doing this, you are managing expectations – this not only will keep you out of trouble, but will give your words the power of leadership, that comes with your own reputation for clean reliability.

****

Now one more thing about promissory liability. It not only arises as the platform upon which you deliver words. Promissory liability is also the platform upon which you receive authority or power granted to you.

When you are granted authority over how to spend some one else's money, by receiving this authority you accept a promissory liability to spend it, disburse it, according to the instructions received by the giver of the funds. By your receiving this authority, your are agreeing and accepting the limits of the terms for its use, for its purpose.

Here promissory liability is not created by the act of what you say, but reliance on you is induced by your act of accepting what someone else has given to you. This is the person or corporation, or government giving to you a certain power or authority, saying to you in any fashion, as to what is the controlling purpose for your being given this power and authority.

When you receive and hold any power and authority from another, you have promissory liability imposed on you, to use it for the purpose it was given.

And when you use it for a purpose not intended, you will be deemed "corrupt". All your life you are gong to hear the word "corruption".   You may never have taken a moment to figure out exactly what this means. Well, here is that moment:

"Corruption" as a word, has a precise content.

It means the act of a person who uses the power, the authority or the money given to him for a purpose different than intended.

Simple. Divert the money or authority given to you for a purpose not intended, and you are entering an arena where you can be called "corrupt" - whether you were aware or not at the time of occurrence.

Most of the time, "corruption" is used with respect to people in government. This is because every manager in government is using money and authority granted to them which is based on a specific purpose stated in written law or regulation.

Similar diversion of company funds for purposes unrelated to the original intent, is also an act of corruption and a cause of promissory liability for those who accepted authority to disburse funds.

Bottom line, again: - incidents creating promissory lability can be like weeds growing in your front lawn. They can easily appear without warning when you are not paying attention, and ultimately will force your dealing with them. They will occur as a consequence of a failed awareness of how your words and acts affect other people. It is a phrase easily remembered.

Keep these words "promissory liability" as a flashing beacon to guide you away from the shoals of avoidable and damaging consequences in your life's journey.

Chapter 21

Is it in your nature to be a Professional?

Do You Want to be a Person Who is Trusted?

You would be this kind of a person ...

Following every human tragedy you see on television media, there comes quickly a group of people clustered around a microphone. They announce themselves as first responders to the horrible event. Praise and gratitude is properly bestowed. But the "thank you's" are met with an insistent response that "we are professionals."

Lawyers and Medical Doctors call themselves professionals. The buildings in which their offices are clustered, are called Professional Buildings.

"Professional" is a term that people find highly desirable when talking about themselves and what they do. Even bankers want to be called "professionals", as well as those in occupations that require performance in technical and physical management.

It would seem to be natural for you, at the beginning of your voyage into the impersonal world of human beings, to look to the future and see yourself known as a professional in whatever career you would choose - not just doctors, lawyers and architects and accountants, but professionals in construction, marketing, insurance, whatever involves you with people.

If you are going to be making money during your life, you will of necessity be dealing with people. The exceptions are rare, such as day trading in stocks, or panning for gold by your lonesome self.

So your life time spent on making money in some way, will require your dealing with people in some way. Earning money is, by and large, a people relationship activity - involving mutual awareness of each other as individuals.

Before you travel too far down this road, you ought to have some clear ideas of how you would like to be thought of and regarded by the people whose lives you will touch with your money making efforts.

This is important, because the amount of time you will be giving to making money, will occupy an enormous part of your conscious life on this planet. You want to make your time worthwhile in every way, not just collecting money.

The relationships you will have, should not be limited to just dealing with what it takes to get money into your bank account.

The huge amount of time that will be carved out of your life to acquire money, should get you something that is more than mere money. As you know, your life speaks to needs that go far beyond money acquisition.

Your relationship to people that happens in the process of making money, is the key to making this time spent more fulfilling to your life, more rewarding to what turns you on.

The key would be to deliberately position yourself as a professional in what ever you do.

It is hard to think of any activity that involves other people that would not be enhanced by your offering your work as the product of a professional. Absolutely just about every activity is elevated by the claim to be "professionally" done.

Exactly what does the term "professional" add to the portrayal of yourself? What does this label do, to make yourself a more desirable person to be employed - to be engaged - by other people?

There are clearly two things you publicly commit to, in saying you are a professional:

1) To claim you are "professional" is to say that you have the knowledge and capability to be trusted to know how to provide a particular service to the highest standards known, and

2) Further, to claim you are a professional is to communicate that you can be personally trusted and depended upon to see that this high level of service is provided, at all times even to the extent of putting your client's interest ahead of your own.

3) You let people understand that you will decline to do the job, unless you know you can meet that standard of excellence that you have set for yourself and have caused others to expect from you.

When you say you are a "professional", you are effectively asking people to depend on you to do something for them, that they cannot do for themselves. You want them to trust you personally to fulfill their need.

You want a relationship that holds the respect for yourself that supports this trust. You must conduct your relationship in a manner that people see you as expecting this trust in yourself.

But professional trust is not just about getting a job done. There is a special expectation here. It is about you taking upon yourself to create the best possible outcome that can be humanly done. A professional takes great pride in being so trusted. He takes pride in that expectation.

This is what professional work means - being trusted to create the best possible outcome. - and then performing - delivering a result that befits this trust.

Even when you are young and starting work, there is everything right about your creating this expectation, in just simply saying to your boss: "Trust me, I will do a great job for you." For sure, he has seldom heard this from a young person. He will remember you.

But if you can not promise an excellent outcome due to your own limits, or for whatever reason, it would be part of your professional stance to be frank, and say so.

This has to be something that you should consciously want: To be trusted to give people the best in doing things for them that they cannot do for themselves.

In creating the highest reliance on yourself, you will also create for yourself great and enduring relationships around your ability and your determination.

And you should take pride in creating this expectation - that you will be recognized as a professional.

You are a professional - when "rely on me" is your personal call to the world - and then you make the best that can happen, really happen to everyone that trusts you. For yourself, you will have a very personal satisfaction that comes in no other way.

To be known as a person that people trust, is a compliment you should look for. When this happens, you will know that you are as close to the heart of everyone's goodwill as you can ever be.

Chapter 22

GOVERNMENT - Corking a Violent Volcano -

Your private thoughts about public government

You already know about Government. It's everywhere. Government is boring.

But as you take off after becoming 18, you should have some basic idea in your pocket of what Government means to you, if anything.

Yes, you probably agree. "But not now" would be a normal response. However, you are already reading this page, so let's do it now. In five minutes you may have a different idea of Government that will underlie your thoughts for a lifetime.

Like the ground beneath you, everywhere you go on land, you expect the ground to be there. Same with this thing called government. It is so everywhere, you don't pay much attention to the fact that it is - everywhere. So you never get to see what it is like, when Government is not around your life.

So what's it like when government is not around? It is the flip side of boring. Very exciting.

Government is a plug. It is a plug in a huge volcano. This volcano is never dormant. Sitting In place, this is the most boring of plugs. But when it gets loose and weak, leaks or breaks down, all hell breaks out.

Inside this volcano, lies the eternally hot magma of red liquid rock that aptly describes what the plug of government is hiding and controlling: this is the spilling of blood - human blood.

Human Beings - that's us - left by ourselves to be free to deal with each other's free will, engage inevitably in instant conflict, and constant physical destruction of each other's property and lives.

It is a fact. Where no single controlling force exists, constant uninhibited conflict is a fact. Check your memory of all the human conflict in whatever history you have learned.

You will remember reading of the constant physical war of humans on each other in pursuit of material needs for survival, in seeking revenge of perceived wrongs, in imposing punishment and justice, in satisfying lust and desires for enjoyable riches held by others. It is instigated by individual humans pursuing that human yearning of doing whatever it takes to bring power to one's personal existence to fulfill underlying desires for the praise or fear of other human persons.

Throughout the history of almost every society and civilization, we encounter the same response to this human created violence. It is an organizing principle that repeats itself in all kinds of human groupings. It is in response to the first rule of life we all instantly understand. This rule is that we first must survive. In direct response to this rule of survival first, comes the one necessary principle we all have recognized for the mutual protection of humans living together.

The principle is this:

We must live - all of us - under a Government Organization that holds a monopoly on physical coercion.

So what does this mean? Look around you. Who has the power to cart your body off and put it in a cage? Only the Government can put you in prison. If anybody else tries this, it is a crime of kidnapping with severe punishment.

Wherever your body goes, you go. So the Government and only the Government today can abduct you, confine you by force to be separated from your friends and family. In other words, put you in jail. Only Government can do this. No other power is allowed to touch your body without your consent.

Your money in the bank: Who has the power to take your money? Only the Government has this power. Nothing but Government can touch it. And it can do so, only by way of it being granted a monopoly on physical coercion.

Who can throw you out of your own house and home, because you owe money? Your bank cannot do this. None of your creditors can do this. The only way they can possibly take your house, or any of your property or possessions, is to ask the Government to do it - for them, by physical force, on their behalf.

And so you end up in Court, where the Judge represents and holds the power of the Government's monopoly on physical coercion. He decides the use of this power. Under it, the judge can take away from you any or all of your possessions.

The Government gives the Judge certain rules to follow in doing this. These rules are the laws that the Government enacts for this purpose through its legislature. It is all done under this principle that is rarely spoken out loud: that Government holds a monopoly on physical coercion.

Who can force you to drive on one side of the road, and not the other? And how fast, or how slow? And what clothes you can take off in public? No one can touch you and physically force you to do these things in a particular way. But on any day, Government can physically grab you by the collar, and through its granted monopoly on force, it has the ability to physically cart your body off to jail, if you do not conform to the rules it sets. And only Government can do this.

So your first idea about Government is simply this: Government is force. Government is all about physical force. Only Government can use this force.

Government can be involved in every human activity. It can tax and build great projects, and regulate your garbage. But all Government activity begins with its ability to use physical force, and ends only when it loses this physical force.

Every society - by its own choice or by imposition - has lived with a presence of a physical force, capable of controlling every individual's conduct.

Much of history show human society having this physical force imposed from Conquerors outside of it, or from Dictators within. The Roman Empire conquered and governed most of Europe for centuries. When it ended, its monopoly on physical coercion ended. The so-called Dark Ages then began, with the chaos of help-yourself violence ensued and descended on the region for ensuing centuries.

In response to this, History also shows societies over time voluntarily creating their own organization they call Government, and to which they have voluntarily granted this same monopoly of physical coercion to keep peace and order.

So then, consider this: when societies got rid of conquerors that ruled them with physical force, they went ahead and created their own organizations and gave them the same monopoly power to use this same physical force on their own people - but with rules to prevent abuse.

So you conclude rightly, that people do not want to live without there being a designated holder of a monopoly power of physical coercion being in place.

Why is this true? It all comes down to survival. Human survival - surviving each other's individual personal free will- requires this. In all societies - whether the sensate society of animals or the free will society of humans - the need to survive is most often the source of all rules of conduct that are found to be universally present.

This is easy to understand: that within a society of humans we must have an organization that has a monopoly on physical coercion. We call it a "Government". This is how the state of peace within a society is kept. Government steps into all human conflict that breaks out into forcing and fighting, and stops it. It is the cork in the volcano of human conflict.

Without this capping of human conflict, we could never have a thriving commerce where people can trade and make a living. Business requires government to keep the peace - that makes business possible.

So as you become someone involved In business, you want government, you need government. You support Government.

This grant to Government of a monopoly of physical coercion is a good and necessary choice. Getting every one to understand this, is not a problem.

But then it gets complicated. Because here is the central problem of Government, and where all further agreement tends to break down:

How do you control this granted monopoly of physical coercion that Governments must have to stop the constant human conflicts that destroy peace and disrupts living?

As a practical matter, how do you contain this awesome power? Well, No one has ever had a perfect answer to this, and never will.

There are no philosophical answers, because there are no philosophical questions here.

This is just a real practical problem: How do you control the power that peace requires?

There are no principles or ideals that will guide us to a solution. It is not that kind of a question.

All answers are strictly nothing more than pragmatic solutions - meaning what ever works.

Under the heading of "whatever works", comes this practical idea of giving control of the needed monopoly power of physical coercion to people who are selected by a majority of votes of those who will be subjected to this monopoly. These same voters can then take away the granted power, if they see abuses, and vote in their replacements.

This practical solution for controlling these monopoly holders of force (called Government) by a majority vote of the people subjected to it, is called "democracy".

But it is not a clean solution. For instance, the troubling weakness is that those granted this monopoly power, can use its coercion to tax. And so they raise money to reward the majority of voters to ensure their continued vote for themselves - the incumbents. Once this power is granted by majority vote, it can become really difficult, sometimes impossible for those not in the majority to remove the majority - in a pure democracy.

There is nothing inherently moral or right about any decision of a majority of voters. It's not a principle. It's just a number, an arbitrary number like in the rules for a winning hand in a card game.

So as a practical matter, Democracy is not enough of a safeguard against the abuse of the monopoly of power that Government must hold to make society livable. Democracy by itself, it is not a solution. And this has been well recognized.

So the people on this planet trying to make democracy work have generally agreed on the need to add one further practical step, that seems to work in most nations for controlling those who hold the monopoly power of physical coercion.

The one further step is this: We list the important rights that people want to always exist, and definitely do not want a democratic voting majority to be able to change. We also list the rules for organizing and legislating the use of government power, that also we do not want to allow a democratic voting majority to change.

Then we put these lists in a written document that will contain a rule that these basic rights and rules cannot be changed without a super majority of votes taken under time measured conditions and controls. We call this document a Constitution.

If the Constitution could be changed by a simple (democratic) majority of votes, then there would be no point in even bothering with such a Constitution. When you allow a simple majority to control everything, you give away all protection to prevent basic rights and principles from changing. So if you can make Constitutional changes by a majority vote, there is no Constitution. If everything is allowed to change by vote of a simple majority, then everything is open to change on these terms. Simple majority dictates.

This obvious exposure to the raw power of a simple majority is what drives the need for a written Constitution containing lists of basic rights and rules that must be resistant to change.

But there is immediately a further problem. This Constitution must then contain provisions for its own resistance to change This is everywhere done mostly by a requirement of super majorities.

This two step practical solution of controlling a government, first by majority voting, and then, secondly, by a written Constitution, is called a Constitutional Democracy.

This is used by the United States, and many other nations. No two are exactly alike. In the United Kingdom they have no written constitution. They effectively accomplish the same restraints by the supervision of their Courts applying customary Rules of Law.

Oddly, what is a practical solution to controlling Government's monopoly power in one country, can be quite different in another. Each nation has to deal with the fierce loyalty of its culturally bound tribal groups, and the temperament of its people. Temperament can be driven by their genetics.

Temperament Is an important consideration in the process of decision-making in public, even though voting is done privately. The difference in temperament in dealing with contested issues, can require different practical steps in trying to obtain an individuals real thoughts into controlling his vote. Different Temperaments in different cultures can vary from instant high emotions in response to frustrated desires, to calmer responses facing the same frustrations or desires.

So by sheer reason of different temperaments in people coming from commonly held genetics or culture, nations vary in their ability to use democracy and constitutions to control their government's needed monopoly on physical coercion.

Democracy - even a Democracy with a written Constitution - is not an effective answer for many nations. And never will be. The format of a government in the Middle East nations may look like Constitutional Democracy. However, its real life workings may be driven by the character of real life relationships of a people in their own world, quite different to what would be going on in nations like the United States, Italy, or France.

A key element in this Constitutional document is that it contains provisions that its content can not be changed by a government's elected officials. It can only be changed by significantly more than a majority of voters who must meet together in separate and formal circumstances designed to slow down any rush to change, and to impose time for argued consideration.

It is intended that those who are voted into government office in a Constitutional Democracy, will be chained to a written Constitution document limiting their power.

But even so, the stability of a written Constitution, requires a continued voluntary affirmation by those already holding government power. Like a torch it is handed by one generation to the next in good faith that it will remain lit. It is always as fragile as the hands that now hold it against the winds of trouble.

Every generation will have its own special challenge in hanging on to the apparent stability of written constitutions. And in every nation, the efforts will be different.

But all will be looking for new solutions. In our present computer oriented world of attempting to use protocols to manage such human problems, it has become a trend to try to rely on process to control the free will endowed humans on this planet. You will see many versions of this futile protocol effort during your lifetime - both in government and in business.

This scheme of democracy - a majority in voting restricted by a constitution in writing - seems to work in many nations. But even this practical solution, this

Constitutional Democracy, has its limits. It is not going to work well in places where the population does not have a patient temperament to acquire awareness of what's going on with their government, and vote with this awareness after some consideration. Democracy does not do well in highly emotional populations.

In societies where disputes and disagreements create immediate and highly emotional responses, patient consideration is a lost cause. People's responses to conflict and fear are genetically shaped and culturally practiced. In these places democracy would not ensure stability. The democratic format can be created, but the reality of what will really happen as a consequence, will be genetically and culturally based.

Nevertheless, such countries are pressured from the larger nations to have some form of a voter based democracy. And while they may comply and go thru the charades of appearing to have a democratic process, their present society will not be entirely with it. It will take generations before this effort, can come to some accommodation with culture and genetics.

Why then, if democracy is so inherently imperfect, do nations like the United States, treat it like an "ideal of civilization", which it is not? Well, there is a practical side to all this pushing and idealizing and celebrating democracy as the ideal form of government.

Democracy - voting majority deciding- is also sold by praising the possibility of everyone having a say in the use of government power. This is appealing to a "feel good" label, even though an immediate second thought to a thinking person, is that democracy is definitely not a "feel good" event for the losing 49% - people not in the majority.

But a supporting argument is that democracy responsive to a majority, best furthers the basic mission of government to prevent humans from engaging in self-help physical coercion.

A Government - controlled by democratic majority voting - is by this means, more likely to deal with emerging and serious dissatisfactions before deep frustration can turn into violence. This helps to keep a cap on human conflict.

But, there is a major reasoned reality behind this popularized (tongue in cheek) selling of democracy world wide as a public virtue and ideal. This urgent reality has nothing to do with the adequacy of democracy as a means of controlling and guiding government's use of its fundamental powers of physical coercion.

Everyone watches this constant public cheerleading by Nations, like the United States, continually pushing democracy on old societies, however incompatible with their ancient traditions and their own ethnic genetics.

If you asked how reasonable is this, you will likely get this quiet answer:

It is a hard fact, that governments run by democracies, seldom initiate serious wars against other nations, and their capacity to continue such conflicts is lessened.

Dictators, not having democracies, can more easily bring their country to war. Democratic leaders of a nation, have a more complicated government system - constant disagreements of a voting population are readily voiced. Leaders in a democracy would have immediate approval problems in preparing for a war.

A democracy is recognized to be the least likely form of government to start a war of aggression against other nations.

So in the well meant effort to foster peace throughout the planet, nations like the United States, and organizations like the United Nation, keep pushing democracy on every nation at every opportunity, where ever they can. The more people that are occupied with democracy, the less people will be occupied with war. This is a basic premise in their missionary effort for peace.

But in appreciating this agenda effort, there is no reason to be caught up in the notion that democracy is actually some sacred ideal, when, more profoundly, and first and foremost, democracy is simply a practical solution to controlling the monopoly of physical coercion that governments must possess to keep society civilized in peace. Democracy is not a sacred element of morality. It is just a practical judgment of how best to make a society of humans survive and work together.

Bottom Line - as you go through life witnessing the activities of Government around you, be considering this:

Understand Government, is meant to be an overwhelming organized Force.

When forming a Government your purpose is to create force, and create a control of that force. It's all about force.

George Washington, the first President of the United States, was part of putting that new Government together from scratch in the late1700's. He knew what he was dealing with. He said: "Government is not reason; it is not eloquence; it is force. Like fire, it is a dangerous servant and a fearful master."

Understand Government as society's single holder of the power of sheer physical force.

It has a monopoly on physical coercion in your everyday world.

All forces are inherently dangerous.
Government is inherently dangerous

No force is inherently benign - kindly if left alone.
Government is not inherently benign.

All power when confined, resists confinement.
It inherently tries to escape.
Government is physical power confined by limits of a democracy and a constitution for most of the world in our present time.

Government inherently will try to escape its confines.

All forces require attentive management, in other words, keep aware of what it is doing.

Two words to keep in mind in any power of force management: Vector and Velocity.
Watch where it is going, and at what speed.

Any force can be weaponized to destroy.
Government Power in any form or function, is a highly attractive weapon.

All the political arguments you will ever have in your lifetime, will center around the use of this unique monopoly on force that only government possesses. So in your political discussions go to this bottom line, and lead the conversation to speak in terms of this force of government, and it will lend the clarity of focus to your disagreements.

Politics and economics will intertwine in discussion about government throughout your life. Capitalism is not so much a subject about economics as it is a subject about when, where and how to use or restrain the physical force that only government uniquely possesses, in its application to economic activity. The same is true in discussions of socialism, and communism. It all ultimately centers on a different extended use of a government's monopoly on physical coercion into a society's economic activity.

All kinds of people have all kinds of ideas to take advantage of the existence of this ready made force monopoly for all kinds of further uses. It is so neatly already in place, it is hard for people to keep their hands off of it.

Inevitably, people outside of Government will try to bend this power of Government to their own personal use. Individuals in government regulated businesses will constantly attempt to use government's regulatory power to limit their own business competition, and to create conditions that increase their profits. You will learn to look for these buddy relationships between the regulated and the regulators.

You - and all your fellow humans – need an operating Governments for everyone to live well, and that means living in peace. You absolutely need Government force, and therefore it must be given an affirming respect.

But at the very beginning of discussing and dealing with government, understand Government as that necessary plug in a volcano: keeping people from resorting to violence in the inevitable conflict of their free wills - the human volcano.

In general attitude -

Tell yourself that you can never afford to be disengaged from the management of Government.

Never take its stability for granted.
Never take your eyes off the activities of Government.

Treat Government with caution - like a huge dam silently holding back the power of a large body of water, an enormous force- below which you live.

Chapter 23

Resolving Conflicts - Looking to the Future

How to think about a Lawyer

Trying to live without ever, ever getting wet?

You have about as much chance of succeeding in this, as you do in avoiding a trip to a Law Court sometime during your life.

And it is in a law court room that you will likely first confront the power of the government's monopoly on physical coercion, other than being brought to a sudden stop by a police car.

You can easily be forced to enter a court room.

Someone just has to claim that you did something that offended the rights of one of your fellow humans, or you violated one of the laws or regulations of your Government. A complaint is filed, and you can be compelled to walk through a court room door.

In other words, your conduct in doing something, is claimed to be in conflict with the laws and rules of the society you're living in. So you are hauled into a place called a Court Room, where you come face to face with an organization that holds a monopoly on physical coercion over you and every one in your country - personally. It is your Government, of course, and the face of it, is a person sitting above you, behind a high desk.

We call this person a "Judge". He holds a power of physical coercion over you. Nobody else around you holds that power. To make sure that everyone understands this, he will wear a black robe. Sit in an impressive chair with a high back, reminiscent of the thrones that kings have used in the past. The room will likely be decorated with well known symbols of authority, mostly from the Roman Empire that past Kings and Conquerors have also used. You will recognize them as depicted in all your history books.

All of this is deliberate theater. It is done to prepare you to accept the Judge's power, and the use of his power to control you, if he finds it necessary. This is a contrived setting to impress everyone who enters a Court room. But this theatrical effort and the reason for it, is something you should understand. Because when you enter a Court Room, theatrics aside, the physical power over you is real.

But in being a level headed person, you will have no resentment. You will understand that the monopoly of physical power which the Courts hold as Government, is necessary; and you can also understand that the theater which the Courts create to display this power, helps to encourage its acceptance, and the peaceful settlement of your disputes.

So the Courts are the day to day engine of Government to keep a lid on the constant play of conflicts in people's daily lives.

Through its monopoly of physical coercion, government gives people only two choices to resolve conflicts that they cannot manage to quell themselves. They must walk away from problems they cannot resolve, or bring them to a Court, where a Judge will decide,

The Judge's decision will be enforced by an Order he will issue to other Government officials to use physical coercion on people to make them do exactly what his Order requires. This can result in non-complying individuals going to prison, or having their property, or money seized and distributed to other people - all according to the Judge's decision.

Bottom line: This "Court forced" resolution of conflict is made possible by Government's monopoly on physical coercion. This daily work by the Courts create a manageable playing field for everyone's day-to-day living in relative peace. It keeps the engines of commerce going undisrupted.

So your attitude towards these Courts, as you go through life, should be based on this understanding. You will want to be genuinely supportive. It is hard to earn a living in a society that is continually upset and in an uproar over unresolved conflicts. Courts settle these disputes, and everyone's life goes on.

But knowing that a day will come when you will find your own self in a Court Room, you should take a moment, pause and stall, and think ahead. From your last day in school you should have an awareness to be on the lookout for a lawyer you may want to use, when sudden events will create a sudden need.

You will be looking for a good attorney. Selecting an attorney requires judgment. Judgments are seldom done well when you are in the hurry of instant trouble. The need for an attorney to often arises too abruptly.

So creating a relationship with an attorney is something to have considered in advance.

Two points in this consideration:

Lawyers like doctors, are increasingly confining themselves into specialities. They all know their own limits, and most will be aware of who are the capable people in other areas. Ask your chosen lawyer about his willingness to direct you to other lawyers if needed. This will be your way of educating him that you are a discerning client that expects results. This is one of those initial by-the-way things to say that creates important attitudes.

In the end, you will find yourself thinking that there will be only two kinds of lawyers handling your problems: great lawyers and possibly dangerous ones. You have to think about how you can tell the difference.

Beside asking and receiving adequate information about his experience, you will have to depend on your own judgment with a focus on concerns noted here.

In discussing a problem, if a lawyer only seems to be lecturing you about the content of a certain law, leaving you to figure and chose the outcome, this academic soul should not be your lawyer. You want to see your chosen lawyer worrying about outcomes for you, initiating discussion about the goals that you want, and how best they can happen. Then that person should be your lawyer. Be decisive about this, and follow your hunches.

By the time you are 22 or 23 years of age, you should have a lawyer selected. You do not have to be in trouble to get this done.

I was amazed to find how clearly young people sense this. Teaching in an MBA program for a university, there were always instant visitors in the classroom when the announced topic was "How to hire and fire a lawyer, and provide the leadership your lawyer needs." Students would bring their friends.

You can tell almost at once, how good a lawyer will be in mastering your problem. You can judge by the effort this lawyer will make in extracting from you every detail of your problem, and every corner of your concerns, before attempting to give you legal advice.

This means that he is trying to understand everything from your point of view, and that he is oriented to be of service in terms of your desired outcomes. You want to see your lawyer doing this. If not, do not hesitate. Find another one that meets this criteria. It will save you money and trouble.

Attorneys who jump in with legal advice before they have made themselves understand the full context of your concerns, are doomed to disappoint you. They may know the law, but they will not fully understand what needs to be addressed in your total context. Best not to get involved with attorneys who are not service oriented. You can judge this by observing how carefully the attorney may be in trying to understand the details of your concerns. This is the reason that you want to hear him voluntarily ask about the results, the outcomes, you need in solving any problem. That would be an attorney you can trust. He cares about you. His work will be caring oriented.

Finally, a practical note: insist that you be given a copy of all the paperwork generated. Why? It is a precaution that simply honors your growing sense of living in a human world where there are no guarantees - where anything can happen. Possessing copies of your own legal files will give you freedom and independence going forward. This is important if you have to change your legal counsel, or he is no longer around when you concerns come up again.

Just let yourself be comfortable with the law processes around you. Avoid fear and awe. A lot of Law Stuff is mostly common sense attention to a world of rules, and the mystery is nothing more than getting used to a different vocabulary. But It is a needed world, and its landscape should be a familiar part of your nearby terrain.

Going back centuries, the needed monopoly on physical coercion was usually held by a person who was a King, So then when you needed use of the government's power, to settle a conflict or get a benefit, you would search for someone who had access to the King. It would be one of the King's friends, or relatives, or appointed assistants. You gave him a gift to use his access to the King to plead your cause and get a favorable response.

We don't have operating Kings anymore. Organized bureaucratic governments who are expected to operate on reason and law, have replaced them. But the tradition of using people with access to power persists today. These friends of the King are now professional advocates to whom we give the title of Lawyer or Attorney. They plead your cause, your needs, to the holder of the monopoly of physical coercion which is now an elected government, and not a king.

For the most part, the things you need from a lawyer, getting a contract arranged, an agreement worked out, obtaining a permission needed from government, getting retribution for injuries, getting relief from abuse, all of these involve getting the backing of the government's monopoly on physical coercion, if they are to be outcomes that will successfully occur.

Everything must be done so that a Government Court can be used to enforce your needed results. Courts will enforce agreements, order compensation for injury, enjoin abuse, and ensure that permissions obtained from government stay in place.

It is the lawyer's job to fashion solutions to your needs, that ultimately a court will support and ensure by force.

So lawyers today still have the basic same old and ancient job description of being connected people pleading your needs to the King. But in place of a King you can now expect a democratically elected government holding that monopoly power of physical coercion. Lawyers no longer get gifts from their clients for their work with kings. They require fees from you. As in past history, a lawyer's service has never been considered to be a light expense when dealing with the ultimate physical power in your society.

But today there is more reason for this. Lawyers are not just hired for their useful connections to the holders of the government monopoly of physical coercion. Much more is required now to deal with government power. They need to be educated about the government's use-of-power rules - today more complex than one King could ever hold in his crowned head.

Certification of their knowledge of government rules for the use of this power is required in passing a Bar Examination - given by the Government itself. So the job is more complex, although it is just the same old profession of representing people in their dealing with a King, as the holder of the monopoly of physical coercion in their society.

Bottom line: having lawyers around is how you get your own personal access to the government monopolized control of physical coercion for your own benefit.

The need for lawyers is the price we pay for being able to live in a nation that is civilized. The lawyers are the instruments we use to employ our government's monopoly on physical coercion to control and resolve our inevitable conflicts in a society of free persons, each with a dynamic free will.

It is through the use of lawyers that we are enabled to acquire and keep what we need and what we possess in a peaceful manner, avoiding exposure to violence in settling conflicts. This use of lawyers works in spite of its occasional failure and corruption.

Think of the alternative. Imagine what you would have to do, if the lawyer system was not in place.

The cost of chaos and disorder in the competition to access government power for your own needs, would be unbearable.

Chapter 24

Showing You are not a Simple Mind

A Scientific Proof

This is a discussion that is off the main road. So put your curiosity in four wheel drive.

What we are about to discuss is some thinking you should now experience. Then lock it in your memory for future use. Not only because it is the right thing for yourself. But it will help you to stand out in a confused world.

Dazzling new things have been happening to humans since the 1950's. Life changing scientific advances have knocked back very basic and accepted limitations on human living. It has happened at a pace never before experienced by people living on this planet.

Look at what astonishing new capabilities have come to reality in the lifetime of those around you:

233

- in the 1950's - The arrival of passenger jets - cruising to everywhere at 500+ miles per hour. So began the ability for a human person to move to any populated area on the planet within 24 hours.

- in the late 1960's - Humans landing on the moon. Outer space travel.

- in the 1970's - The emergence of instant mutual awareness everywhere on earth by satellite television.

- in the 1980's - The creation and placement of computers in everyday workplaces that reorganized and connected worldwide business operations.

- in the 1990's -The establishment of an Internet of instant access to all of the world's knowledge wherever a computer was placed.

- In the 2000's, the next ten years, the first decade of the 21st century, the spread of mobile instant communication between persons everywhere, at anytime, to anybody, was made possible by new electronics that made cell phones massively usable.

What happened next was astonishing even in the context of these recent amazing advances.

In 2007, a technological advance occurred that gave human striving a tool for productivity of their powers beyond any dream that humans had ever conjured, hoped for, imagined, much less ever thought possible. In all recorded history, there was never even a thought of it being possible until just a short few years before it happened.

It paralleled in a sense what Henry Ford did in the early 1900's, almost a century ago for the human body. He did not invent the automobile. Henry Ford's design and production technique made possible the mass produced car that people could afford, and quickly people everywhere became free to transport their bodies as they desired.

.
But what about transportation of the mind?. People want to go places with their minds, even more urgently then they want to transport their bodies.

In 2007, Steve Jobs led his Apple engineers to advance the design of the computer and the cell phone, to make the Internet - all of mankind's stored and current knowledge - available on a small personal display that every human person could carry in their pocket and use on the instant to access knowledge everywhere - whether from a stored document or a living person. He named it the iPhone.

Suddenly - everyone had instant transportation available for their minds to all the world's going knowledge - an instant access, day and night.

The travails of traveling the world for needed knowledge, at great expense of time and money, were over. These barriers are gone. Everyone can now research and know instantly. Anyone with an active mind has the whole world presented to him or her on the instant of a convenient moment. A mind is no longer limited to where the body is located. Never has such opportunity been given to such a vast number of people - particularly young people to test their own new ideas and to discover new ones. Now it only takes the initiative of their own self direction.

The iPhone and later the iPad, have set the mind free.

For decades now, humans have lived lives immersed in these wow factors of scientific advances. They have no experience of living in a world less stimulating and where excitement from science is not blurring their common sense about it.

So then there is this down side to these decades of incessant stimulation and excitement: It leads naturally to a giddy mindset accepting easily the thrill of whatever is said to be scientifically based and new.

However, a giddy mindset leads to gullibility. The gullibility is the willingness to accept as inevitably true and real, every announcement of any thing new and amazing from a scientific or technical authority - whether it is about the weather here on Earth, civilizations on other planets, quantum physics, or the effects of drinking coffee, or eating broccoli.

Because the word science is used in the story, there is a presumption of belief and unquestioned credibility. And why not? Living in a world where so many amazing things are predicted and then become real, you are not inclined to question science. Most people will not. Old or young.

Throughout your life, you will hear about new scientific advances. Everything said to be new, is immediate and urgent news for the media. And so you will be drawn into a casual conversation of unquestioning acknowledgment of claimed-as-new scientific advances, findings, and discoveries.

But the conversations will usually not include questioning or critical thinking of assertions by scientists. It is seldom heard and is not of any popular interest. You will easily have little more to say at age 25, than you would have at age 15 - just gawking and accepting. Generations ago, the popular presumption was to be skeptical, and that inspired critical thinking.

At the present time, in light of all that has happened, the popular presumption only asks you to be accepting and cheering. There is nothing to encourage you to be a critical thinker of the new scientific offering of each new week or month.

You could easily be just another simple minded, accepting person, giving fast food approval to everything said to be the consensus of scientists.

Or, you could be somebody who has a thoughtful mindset on the wow topics of new science - a mindset that reacts with perceptive questions to ask, and an awareness that avoids giddy and easy agreement.

This mindset would reflect someone who knows how to think. As a young person, you want this reputation. You want people to learn to listen to you. You help yourself immensely by having thought in advance about subjects that you know will keep coming up in everyday conversations.

In this thoughtful mindset about new scientific advances, your reaction in these conversations should be a straight forward question, and it is simply this:

Are we talking here about some scientific finding that has been proven, or are we talking about scientific speculation?

Big difference between science that is speculating about a happening or consequence that can occur, and science that is proving that a happening or consequences does in fact occur.

Your mind should always ask If what is being talked about is just speculation, or is this conversation about how an idea has been proved to be real. In a showing of leadership, you should require this answer, before letting the conversation go forward.

Proving something scientifically to be true, is a wholly different effort, than trying to show consequences as if something were true.

When you are working with proving something to be true, you are into observations, measurements, making logical deductions, using reason to predict, and then making repeatable experiments that confirm and show that no other explanation is available to contradict what appears to be true.

When you see this going on, you know you are hearing about an effort in applying scientific method to show something being true. This means you are talking about a "scientific finding."

However, It will be clear to you that you are discussing only scientific speculation (not scientific findings or determinations) when the hot topic is about what is going to happen, what can happen, what is likely to happen, because of some scientific expectation, and yet there is little or no talk of direct proof or other possible explanations that go into any description of a new scientific declaration.

The often used term "scientific consensus" is an oxymoron - meaning a contradictory phrase like cruel kindness. And here, you can accent the word "moron" (ancient Greek for foolish) when this term (scientific consensus) is used to support a scientific conclusion to be trusted. These two words "scientific" and "consensus" do not belong together.

Nothing scientific is determined by consensus.

Consensus is opinion. In the real world, the point of using the word "scientific" is to describe something that is not opinion, but is a hard proven upon a tested finding - not a possible fact.

Both scientists and medical doctors wear white coats. But there is an essential difference in what drives their professional conclusions.

Medical doctors are forced to act on seeing a physical problem that is immediately in front of them. They are compelled to guess and speculate. They live in the fragile world of human life which compels them to make immediate judgments when their knowledge can be incomplete.

Scientists live in a different world where the unproven remains marked as "unknown" until some understanding reaches the status of a scientific finding upon which reliance can be given.

Bottom line is this:
You do not have to take a course in Epistemology (the science and philosophy of knowledge) on a university campus to quickly see the difference in conversation between what science has proven, and what science is speculating.

Scientific speculation is interesting talk about possibilities. This speculation is about something not yet proven to be really and dependably true - not yet a real scientific finding. And it's about possible consequences should it ever be proven to be true.

When you hear the term "computer modeling and simulation" being used, you immediately know that certain and complete knowledge is not available, and that it involves speculation. You will know that this can produce best guesses (uncertain information) but not the certainty of a scientific conclusion. It is the relating of refined estimates to real facts to see the possibilities - not to be treated as certainties.

So if this is the conversation, you know you are still into some speculation. It's about guessing what may be likely.

When the talk focuses on how we would know if some topic of science is true, then we know the discussion is about whether or not a scientific finding is being sought, or has been actually determined. It's about asserting what has been or can be reliably proven, not about what is likely.

This is a basic mindset about scientific topics and discussion. You will want to keep this handy in your pocket. You will be confronted with science conversations, from time to time, all your life.

Be ready to use it in your becoming years, when your ability to show that you are a capable critical thinker, is important to people first meeting you.

Chapter 25

Managing Your Internet Exposure

A 21st Century Essential

Fast and hard is the best way to describe it. This is how young people are being dragged out onto a public stage they never thought existed for them. And twenty some years ago it did not exist. It was not even imagined, much less worried about.

This is the public accessible record of your personal activities. It is the world wide availability of everything you upload to the Internet about yourself, and what your uncontrollable friends will also upload about your life - even your most unguarded moments. Most of this is instantly searchable and will form the beginnings of core information about you. You will have an individual personal public record available to anyone that can type your name- whether you like it or not - on the Internet.

Twenty years ago, young people did not have this problem. Social media to display one's self, interests and relationships, did not exist.

It is there today. You have this public record that builds. It is a file folder that will exist longer than you will. You cannot ignore it, It can affect too much of what people unknown to you, think of you before you've met. It affects the unspoken attitude towards you of those with whom you already deal.

So not being crazy enough to ignore this Internet record of you and your life, there is only one path to take. You have to manage it. This is not being part of the tidy world of people who live by checklists. This management is part of the intelligent energy you bring to master living in the 21st century.

Not too many years ago, young folks just plowed on, confident that they could take care of such issues, if there was ever a reason for an effort.

Now -- Such a stance is just plain stupid (harsh word justified) if you are living on this planet after the year 2000. The Internet reaches down to every person worldwide that has an individual address. The Internet can affect your reputation, even if you never use it much. Other people will mention you. The

Internet presence is like rain. You cannot pretend you're not going to get wet.

The explosion of information technology with limitless permanent storage and instant retrieval of everything put in binary code, has created limitless personal exposure.

Its almost compulsive use by every cluster of humanity, has every digitized detail of your life available for public use. While you may understand how an unfortunate ego hurting record in school came to be, or a low credit score happened, any not-your-fault context will not be there. Explanation is left to anyone's preferred imagination of their worst fears.

This is the result of the flooding everywhere of media devices. Decade after decade the flooding has increased. It is now a permanent feature on the landscape of the living. Since its start, there has been no experience of it slowing down, or even standing still. Growing is part of its essence. No one has ever conceived of the circumstance in which the spreading use of media devices will have stopped. This is a 24/7 reality - like a rising flood that requires being dealt with. It cannot be dismissed. The consequences can be brutal, if it is ignored.

If ignored, you will be a victim of who ever wants to play with your Internet retrievable facts, like a dog shaking its caught little rabbit.

So young people from the year 2000, and forever into the future, have one more basic idea that has to be driven into their heads by those who care about them.

When you were five years old, your primary caretaker had to grab you by the collar and teach you with firm and fierce insistence that you must look both ways before crossing a traffic street. Just as then, when you were from 12 to 18 years old, some caretaker or mentor, should have taken ahold of you, and with the same firm and fierce insistence, taught you to resist displaying your personal stuff on the Internet.

Now, when you are 18 years old and beyond, it will be part of your agenda for survival, to deter, and delete when you can these uploads of your personal activities that could be used against you by a curious but uncaring world.

But your efforts using this same firm and fierce insistence must go way beyond prevention control.

You must consciously go into the web world, as if you were someone interested in hiring you, and wanted to find out everything "possible" about you, and discover yourself.

And "possible" means you have to be smart enough to know what is possible. You must actively teach yourself to see the availability of your self displayed. Get advice. Seek it out, and do not avoid this confrontation. Face it. If you know of someone who is said to be good at searching databases, go to him and ask him to check you out and give you the results.   You will probably be more than slightly astonished.

It used to be that a young person with a normal kind of life, could act reasonably well, and his or her reputation would take care of itself. This is not likely to be sufficient any more - not in the 21st century that is your fated time to be alive on this planet.

Today, friends can easily photograph you in unguarded moments, repeat your off hand comments, uploading to a social web site that is subject to worldwide search retrieval.

And there you stand exposed to a curious possible employer, or anyone wanting to evaluate your nature.

On any given day, your public record may be taking a hit while you are innocently eating lunch or asleep somewhere. And this creates an unasked task for you, because nothing that exists on the Internet, can as a practical matter, ever be easily erased. It would only be taken down by voluntary act of the web site or the person who uploaded, or Court order. You can only ask. The result is out of your control. So you are compelled to do what you can to lessen possible damage.

But there is positive opportunity in carrying this new burden of self protection. With an ordinary effort, you can use this technology to create a positive record of your successes which can also be easily accessed on the Internet.

It takes no effort to realize this. It is another thing to sit yourself down and decide to do now, what you know can be put off forever.

What you can do is take the time and effort to figure out how to put somewhere in the Internet, such information that tells of successes and good experiences that have truthfully been yours. Try to put it in the context of ordinary communication. Search engines will pick these things up regardless of the context that it is in, if you make sure that your usual name is included in the text. Remember that anyone searching for information about you on the Internet, has to begin by putting in your usual name as the object of search. The search results will turn up all contexts that include your spelled out name.

If you put on the web something that favors you but is not the truth, it will inevitably be discovered, disputed, and you will be seen as the foolish author of self promotion. You will be worse off for having tried.

But if it is the truth, no one will care that you might have been the source of it being on the Internet, as long as the self promotion is not obvious.

When your positive information is on the Internet, it will at least have the same presumptive credibility, that the negative bits and pieces of you that find their way into the web. And it will be the needed counterweight to unflattering information which we need to keep reminding ourselves, can never be erased, as a practical matter.

Can you go too far in self promotion? When does good taste, a sense of having some class, restrain your efforts. I asked this of a very famous lawyer when he came to greet me in his anteroom where all must sit who wait for his attentions.

Surrounding on every side of the room, was his picture standing close to some famous political figure or a Hollywood celebrity. There was no empty space anywhere. The walls were crowded with this self adulation.

One picture caught my eye as particularly tasteless, and somewhat unflattering. He was kneeling on one knee suppliantly in front of a seated and very old man, who indeed was Winston Churchill. And the seated Churchill was looking down at him, with the disturbed look of a man who is saying to himself: "what is this?"

Having known this lawyer personally for years, I freely pointed to this photo, and asked if these overloaded and festooned walls might make a tawdry impression on his clients.

His answer was not to be forgotten: "Festooned, yes. Tawdry, maybe. But they will always remember me being with Winston Churchill." And that was a truth. His Churchill meeting event will be remembered, and the tawdry presentation forgotten. But to what end?

An arguable calculation. A result oriented excuse for one's determination to achieve status? It was a memory for me tucked away - thinking there must be limits to what one does to deal with the need for a positive reputation.

How important is it to be proactive in creating a plausibly good picture of yourself on the Internet? How optional? There is a minimum care here that has to be met. And that concerns the fairness of what impression the Internet might be creating of you. This has to be dealt with. You owe this care to yourself and everyone who may have occasion to be conscious of your presence on this planet. Correcting what you consider unfair is that duty you owe, to the truth you know - which is yourself.

At some point, definitely, some people will have questions about you, and they will use the Internet to get answers. It could be a possible employer, a bank loan officer, a school admissions staffer, a possible friend briefly met.

So you want to be proactive - which means that you would take the initiative to ensure that you do have a presence on the Internet. And that there is a searchable narrative of you living your life, that raises no negative concerns.

Why would you want to ensure that you have a presence on the Internet?

There is an additional dimension here, you will want to consider:

The sheer pervasiveness of information technology is now creating its own message.

If you are not found anywhere in the Internet, anyone making a search engine effort will be disappointed, and this lack of any information may not be good for you.

We all learn this at sometime in our lives: reasonable questions should never be left unanswered. Because, then, the wondering has no limits, and negative thoughts are given free rein. Better to provide something for an answer that can dwell in their minds, and foreclose any negative thinking.

Occupying curiosity, is the world's best advice in controlling conversation.

So, on balance, and in line with everyone's expectation in this 21st century, you - now as a young person - should make sure that there is a clear and positive response available to anyone who searches the internet for information about you, and your life's interests and achievements as they occur.

You will have to personally manage this, and when you do, find some one you can trust to mentor your efforts. No one, no matter how old they are, does this well - writing their own biography or image.

Treat social net sites with self-conscious caution. Think ahead of how your input will look in ten years. This is very hard when you are young. Seeing the future in your years of becoming, is really difficult.

Best advice: simply don't drive where you can't see.

Popular social sites invite us to act as if we're all in a present moment. But its moments turn out to be future commitments - even though they are not meant to be a spectacle frozen in time for the ages. But unfortunately this will happen unless you pay attention, and try to control it. It is best to communicate the joys and sorrows of life in text and emails. What you put on a website, you should visualize as being displayed on a billboard along your favorite highway. if you can live with that - that is what you will live with.

Bottom line:

Live in real time consciousness of your personal information on the web. Use the Internet itself to counteract any unflattering items that may be there. Use it to create a positive introduction for yourself.

This is the sort of basic and urgent advice we get when we are taught to look both ways before crossing the street - when we are 5 years old. Anticipate what's coming.

Now in this 21st century with the everywhere Internet growing and media devices proliferating, your on-the-shelf digital reputation is more of a player in your life and your opportunities, than it has ever been in past times.

This has to be paid attention to, just like the solid non-optional rule of looking both ways before crossing a street with traffic.

So now, the new traffic to watch while you cross the streets of your becoming years, is this instant high speed traffic on the Internet.

Just like street traffic, look both ways on the Internet.

Manage incoming and outgoing references to yourself on the Internet with the same everyday concern you would have to take a shower. It is just part of living.

Take an active step by using an Internet search engine to respond to these typed words: - how to remove your personal information from background check.

Whatever street smarts you have, sharpen them to deal with your presence on the Internet.

Chapter 26

HOW DO YOU KNOW - WHO YOU CAN TRUST?

Fundamentals of Trusting People Recently Met

This has never been a problem for you growing up. The question of who you could trust was easy to answer.

You trusted the people who loved you. You knew exactly who to trust. You knew them well. They would be members of your family, and your friends with whom you closely lived.

But, now, after 18 years of being alive, you are about to become immersed in a new-to-you impersonal world. You don't know all the people you will be dealing with. They don't know you.

And yet, now more than ever, you need to have people you can trust around you. A lot of things new are happening to you. You have questions on where to go, who to see, and what you are supposed to do.

Whom do you trust to get the answers you can rely on - answers that would be in your own best interests?

This problem of who to trust? It exists for everyone. You are most vulnerable, when you most need reliable advice and answers. This is when you are young and just starting to dwell in the impersonal world.

When young, you need to depend on your trust in humans around you to get going - like a rocket forced to depend on its first flash of fuel to lift off.

But most young folks, don't think much about it, and just try their luck with people. They do not focus on who to trust because they have no idea what to do about it.

Being 18 and even in their 20's, young persons sort of muff along with their efforts of wondering who can they rely on, being unresolved - taking the hits of mistaken trust as they live from day to day.

But here is a chance to pull yourself to the side of the road, turn off your got-to-go engine, and give this a five minute focused think.

First, consider that this idea of trust begins as something about you, not about somebody else.

You are the one needing this thing called trust. You need someone to turn their attention to you, and think and decide about what is best for you. You need to be able to ask someone a question and get an answer that really considers how best to take care of your own worries and concerns. You are asking somebody to take the time and effort to consider what's best for you.

So in the impersonal world, how do you get people who do not even know you, to be concerned about you?

Well, the answer is, you don't "get" people to do this. There is no getting. The effort is not in getting but in finding - finding people who already want to help you.

You wake up to the idea that there are people everywhere of a certain character and mindset, whom you can readily trust to give you advice and direction in your own best interest - even if they do not know you. How do you know this? You don't. You are simply being told now that this is true. So why not take the chance that it is true. And read on.

If these people exist - and they do - then it is important for you to figure out how you can recognize them, discern who they are.

So then, how do you identify such people?

You must know specifically what to look for. And it is this:

You are looking for persons, who have a nature of being "caring and generous" towards everyone. These two words need to walk together in your consciousness. One without the other, makes both to be empty words - devoid of meaning anything.

You may not have bothered to notice that such people exist. There are humans everywhere who have this built-in attitude of being caring and generous towards the people around them.

You find them by looking for them. You have to start being analytical about the people that enter your daily living. This means pausing to think about them, and evaluate them.

This is a new, and usually unpracticed effort for young persons. When you are growing up every day with the same people, of course, you know them. No reason that you should pause, and think further about them.

So when you now start to look at new people around you, how do you know if a person has this "caring and generous" nature? It is not that hard.

You focus on what you know about that person's relationships. What is said of how he treats his employees, his family, his social friends? A few inquiries on your part, will usually quickly get you answers. You ask people who would know about his relationships. The people that have been part of his dally life, are the ones who would most surely know. You will pick up confirmation in a hurry if such a person is caring and genuinely generous in helping others, not just with money, but mostly with time and deeds. People quickly talk about what they admire in a person.

Caring has a clear meaning. It envisions someone whose concern is naturally engaged, when seeing other humans honestly struggling and needing. Their awareness reaches out to understand the problem and probable solutions. Such a person doesn't have to be asked to be concerned.

This kind of Caring is a natural mindset of people, that from ancient times, and in biblical terms, is known and described as "people of good will."

Being generous is itself a mindset. It is action oriented caring. It is caring that involves depleting one's own resources in contributing what you possess to help another person - whether in time or money.

It is only willing generosity, privately done, that confirms real caring.

When you see generosity in giving, you might be inclined to believe your are seeing an absolute confirmation of a caring person. But quite often this is not true.

People readily donate their resources to projects, people and charities, that will result in personal public praise, their name plaques on buildings, gala dinners celebrating their awards in gratitude. They give to any ego enhancing project that will bring to them public attention, fame and personal gratitude. In this giving, the generosity is about themselves chiefly, and less about caring for other people. This is not the generosity that you can trust.

People around a genuine caring and generous person, will readily speak of his or her private acts of generosity. This is what you must look for, keenly search for. You will be surprised how much you can learn if you make an effort to inquire. The more you try, the better you will be in coming to know who these people are.

This focused inquiry should become a mindset that is a lifelong habit. You will be wanting to surround yourself with caring and generous people, not just to find quickly who to trust when you are young and in need, but to choose whom to live with for an untroubled life.

The "caring and generous" focus in thinking about people and evaluating them, will be an important effort across all of your life's human relationships.

This two word focus works well in wondering about a future spouse. Get to know the intended's brothers and sisters, to see if they speak of a caring and generous person.

What they describe, is likely what you will be getting into, when all the self celebration of wedding is a memory.

When "caring and generous" is absent from your chief understanding of any person, this is a clear warning for you to "proceed with caution".

This is a conscious criteria that should lead all your life's choices in human relationships.

In your bright high-energy years between 18 to 28, it is not unusual for you to think about joining some kind of economic venture with classmates, and friends you happen upon. There is excitement in grouping different talents necessary to a single enterprise. Some don't work out, but some really do. And when they do seem to work, and rewarding money is in prospect, this is when the enthusiasm for each other hits the reality of the personal qualities of each other. You will find things about them you wish you had known before you started.

What you wish you had known, was whether your intended partners had the kind of nature that would want to see everyone rewarded generously, not just themselves.

Thinking about another person's aptitude to being "caring and generous" is a very necessary consideration before you ever join someone with whom you will have a money relationship.

Even though you will want to have entitlement to money worked out and in writing, you will never cover all possibilities of conflict. And even if you could, contracts never solve problems with self-oriented and uncaring people. Better to be forewarned by your assessment of whether you are dealing with a person who has a caring and generous nature. And if not, watch out. You have been warned.

In teaching business school MBA programs, there is a concern to make students conscious of the need to control their business environment with ethical officers and employees. Being "ethical" in business refers to an individual's willingness to be bound by the expectations of what is good behavior in a commercial enterprise. In other words, an individual in the business world is willing to put his complying to these expectations above his own self desires and enrichment when they conflict.

Honestly, it was a task to have the business school students understand the connection between being "caring and generous" and being "ethical"; and how you look for one, to find the other.

You have to pause to think about it. People that are "caring and generous" have a mindset of being able to put the concerns of other people ahead of their own immediate interest. Acts of real generosity always confirm this.

In being considered an ethical person in business, you would be judged as someone that is capable of putting the interests of your company and its expectations for your own behavior, above your own self interests. In other words, in being an ethical person, you would necessarily be some one of a mindset who reaches out to other people's concerns, and who is willing to accommodate their interests.

This is also the mindset of a "caring and generous" person. And this is the reason such people should be highly prized as long term stable partners in any business, or in any joint activity.

So when it come to choosing with whom you will be sharing your economic future, it better be someone known to have a caring and generous deposition.

Bottom line:

Unusual to say, as this may be, this bold first focus on meeting people will save you hours upon hours of grief in your life, from the very beginning of your journey into the impersonal world.   Don't meet people with casual indifference on your part. Be sharp. Be focused. Be wondering: Does this person have a caring and generous nature?

And, of course, there is you. You will want to be seen as having this caring and generous nature in your own self, as the world, one by one, looks you over - as it will.

Put yourself in the mulling crowd - looking at you. Could you be noted as a caring and generous person? Make sure it happens.

Chapter 27

Really Smart Young People Really Need a Mentor

How do you find yours?

We are not thinking here about academic smart - the individuals with the super grades in schooling. They more often want to live pridefully on their academic achievements, and stay with the academic world and it's applauding feedback.

We are concerned about the young person with street smarts. These bright people do not often show up as academic stars. They get decent grades. Their minds aren't captured in the academic world. They are temperamentally more at home in the operating environments of getting things done. They are action oriented - loving to make stuff happen.

Being "street smart" means being smart about the people around you. This means being fully conscious of the individuals one by one with whom you are dealing, and this means being aware of what each person around you is thinking - where their heads are at (in a useful phrase). You think of each individual as a separate universe. This is being "street smart."

This comes naturally to some young people who have grown up with folks who have shown them how it is done, and becomes a copied and acquired talent. Others, not so lucky, have to acquire this essential know-how from some caring older person.

Being street smart means that before you ever confront someone with an attempt to persuade, you look at them with a specific focus. You question in your own mind how this individual is going to instantly react to your persuasion, and you design an effort to connect to his current state of mind.

You don't have to be a genius to figure there is a need to do this. But unless you are a "natural" or have been somehow pushed and trained by a caring adult to this individual oriented awareness, you probably won't be paying attention to the complexity of the individual in front of you. Lacking such street smarts, your persuasive attempts will miss the mark and will fall on unwilling ears, and most often fail.

Without a street smart awareness, you really won't ever be effective with people - getting them to go along with you - whether in organizing people, or keeping yourself organized with them.

But with street smart awareness of individuals around - keeping track of where their heads are at - you, as a young person with energetic work, can easily become a star in your becoming years.

However, there is a danger in becoming successful as a young person. You can become like a shooting star, and quickly wink out.

The reason is easy to understand. No matter how street smart connectable you may be with people, no matter how much energy you bring to work, you can quickly come to the limits of your experience, and therefore of your usefulness.

What people are saying, when they worry that you lack experience to manage a task, is to generally point out that you would be involved in situations where things can be expected to happen, that you cannot be expected to know. Why? Because not all the thinking in the world will help you foresee what cannot be predicted by being logical or being able to analyze. Stuff happens. And you could only know the possibilities from having done it before - in other words, from experience.

Experience takes time. There is no other way to acquire it. When your are young, by definition, you have not had a lot of time to have done many things.

This is why the importance is expressed here of selecting older people that have had the kind of experience and success you wish for yourself, and then deliberately going out and adopting such a person as one of your mentors. Nothing to be ashamed in needing a mentor.

It would show your uncommon good sense and good judgment for you to try to have a personal mentor anytime you are involved in doing things really new to you in environments you have never experienced. It is simply true that the lack of experience does hold back a lot of otherwise capable young people involved in their first projects.

But you never want to accept that a lack of experience can stop you.

There are two ways to handle this:

A normal way would be to stay in line, and work your way through the years to get the experience and acquire the judgment that only experience can bring.

An accelerated way, the best way, the more certain and immediate way, is to adopt an older mentor who has the experience you lack. And join him or her in your efforts.

Ideally, you find someone, caring and generous by nature, whom you would trust. Someone who would take an interest in your concerns. Someone who would have the kind of personal experience you need, and whose approach and temperament you admire.

You will know that someone, when you run across him or her. If it is someone you are fairly certain would be a mentor you would like, use your ingenuity to meet him. If you do not know of anyone who could introduce you, then seek him out in some public forum, he would be attending. You may have to be bold. "Fortune favors the bold" is a proverb that arises for repetition in every generation - for a reason. It works.

You will be surprised how many older people, a full generation (or two) ahead of you, would welcome the opportunity to be a mentor to an energetic young person.

There comes to most every accomplished person, a natural desire to share what they have struggled to learn - particularly if they have struggled. But they are often just as shy of offering their help, as you are of asking for it. It seems to be understood that it is more appropriate for you to be actively seeking a mentor, then the other way around.

One more thing. There is a gift that an experienced mentor can give you that is seldom discussed. And this is attitude.

There was a renowned Professor on Contracts at the University of Chicago Law School, named Malcolm Sharp. All freshman were subjected to him. His beginning lecture was remembered by everyone. "I've been teaching Contracts for over 20 years," he began. "There is no way I can teach you every thing I know about Contract Law in the four months I have you in class. But I will do this. I will give you an attitude toward solving contract problems that should carry you through to solve every conflict you will ever have." And, indeed he did this.

Just in discussing with your mentor, the problems that you are perceiving, inevitably you will get back not just advice, but unspoken attitudes towards handling these problems and conflicts - attitudes and approaches that will be long remembered and become the staple of your own experience.

Perhaps, one day, in grateful memory of those who helped you, you will pass these learned attitudes on to a younger person seeking your help. This, of course, is what is happening here.

But for your own sake there is this to remember in the present moment: the smarter and quicker you are as a young person, the more you will need a mentor in relating to your new world underfoot.

The temptation to overcome is to believe that your own talents and confident understanding, relieve you of this necessity. You must accept that nothing you can imagine, can substitute for experience.

Whenever you are involved in anything that you have never done before, here is the most important sentence that you will ever read on the subject. Carefully look for who in the entire world has the most experience with exactly what you're trying to do, and locate that person and contact that person and ask that person for advice. Do not be afraid to call, or write a letter and ask for a meeting.

You will find most people very willing to share their experience, particularly with honest young persons, honestly inquiring. And assuming there's nothing that suggests that you will be competing with this person, you are more than likely to find advice to be very forthcoming. In other words you will find that most older people are really glad to help younger persons. Count on it and be genuinely grateful for their help.

As a younger person you cannot just sit down and forecast that an older busy person would not be interested in helping you. Respect your limitations. You have never been an older person. You cannot presume to know how they would react to your request.

"Fortune favors the bold." This is how you will find your mentor. Boldly asking.

Chapter 28

Discovering Your Attitude

What Other People Can See in You

When you look in a mirror, you only see one thing - yourself.

When people look at you, they see two two things - yourself and your attitude.

Do you know what attitude people see in you? Doubtful – you never think about it.

But the attitude people see in you, tells them how to deal with you - work with you.

When you are living just in your growing-up world, everyone is already used to how you present yourself. They all know how you operate.

But when you enter the impersonal world, it is wildly different. People do not know what to expect. They immediately search for clues as to what they are dealing with in spending any time or effort with you. They are instantly looking for your attitude in how you may behave in any relationship.

Your attitude, is their first clue.

Would you seem to be an aware and happy person to know and work with? Would you be energetic in getting things done? Would you be understanding? Would you be a person who wants to do things in the right way, with a conscientious concern? Would you make that extra effort to correct something, without being told?

People pick up quickly indications from you that instantly remind them of their prior experiences with other persons. They remember the same little clues from people and their actions that turned out well, or very badly. They will apply this to you, and suspect that you will turnout to be a repeat of their prior experience.

,
All these unspoken questions in meeting you, are so often answered in a flash, as people pick up your

attitudes, in their first few minutes of their first meeting with you.

You will unconsciously present your attitudes.

So this is important for you, as you depart the growing up years where everybody knows you, and enter a world of impersonal people who have never experienced you.

So for the first time in your life, after you become 18, you now have to sharply become aware of your attitudes in terms of how people see them. Because you are going to be more and more immersed in a world of people who do not know you, and you have to be prepared for what they think are your attitudes - not what you think are your attitudes.

The attitudes they will sense about you, will form their first impression of you. Bad first impressions are really hard to overcome.

So how do you discover what kind of attitudes people will sense in you, when first you meet?

Honestly, it will be quite hard to figure out on your own. You cannot ask your best friend. They would know you too well. It would be hard for them to pretend how you would appear, if they did not know you. You could ask a teacher, but still a response would reflect experience with you. But you really want to know what kind of first impression you give. So asking people that already know you, is not going to be helpful.

There is only one other thing that you can do. Take the bull by the horns, decide how you want to appear, and make it happen.

You should decide what attitudes you want people to see in you, and teach yourself to present yourself in that way.

Select the attitudes, that you know you have, and that you would like people to see in you at first glance. Then just remind yourself, when you are first meeting someone, of the way you would like to be understood - that you would like them to see in you.

Generally, having this kind of pre-thought, is all you really have to do. You will naturally speak and act accordingly.

In selecting the attitudes you would like to get across to people you are meeting for the first time, here are some suggestions:

People really reach out to individual humans, who appear to be happy persons. If you first present yourself as a worried, frowning, preoccupied-with-problems type personality, you will find that this is a real turn-off for people. They do not like to relate to problems. They have enough of their own.

Every meeting you have with another human person creates an implicit question of a possible relationship. People go to a happy person like they were a magnet. And like a magnet's other end, people push a way from persons carrying problems on their faces.

So no matter how you actually feel at the moment, let people see you first as a happy person, with a happy face, and a pleasant happy way about you. You don't have to feel happy. Just be happy. Happiness is a choice.

There is a lot of language in a curve - whether it is on an archway, a vase, or a face.

When people see a down curved mouth, they see the unhappy presence of problems, and trouble, and possible turmoil in a person, signaling a burden to share. This invitation is an immediate turnoff.

But in a smile, the curve is up, signaling happiness to share, and a relationship to look forward to, and be pursued. No matter who you are meeting, bringing a sense of happiness with you, is the first thing you want to assure. It makes your presence always inviting and warmly welcomed.

The second most important attitude you want to present is this:

That you are interested in what other people want. You should try to turn the beginning of conversation to what the person you are meeting likes and wants.

This shows that you are interested, as you should be, in understanding the people you meet. And you do this by turning the conversation initially as best you can to a discussion of the likes and concerns of the person you are meeting, not yours.

Only after trying to engage in such a conversation should you bring up your own concerns. This allows people to reflect that you are meeting not just to pursue your own purpose, and this tells them that you are capable of being concerned for the benefit of others - the person you are meeting. This is important. People like to help. But they resist when it can appear that a relationship is being sought just for a self serving benefit.

When they get any sense of being blatantly used, people just turn away - quickly.

Other attitudes which you think ought to be communicated in first meetings, will be guided by your own sense of the moment.

But when you are meeting someone for the first time, and it is about possible employment, I would add one important consideration, to the one just mentioned.

All well managed businesses and projects will have a culture (an ongoing sense) of urgency in their work. They look to bring together as employees, people who by nature are earnest in what they do - trying hard to do well. Your own attitude of earnestness is important to get across, to communicate, to any prospective employer. Forcing an immediate discussion of how many holidays you do not have to work, and how long is 'my' paid vacation, and how many sick days are allowed, suggests an attitude, of wanting to be engaged in work as little as possible. You should know these things, but have the good sense not to use a beginning conversation with an employer on these topics. It suggests an attitude of not being a willing worker.

If you remember to be conscious of the attitudes people can take from what you say to them, you will save yourself a lot of rejection.

Just put yourself in another person's shoes - who is looking at you and hearing you talk. Figure out the attitudes you may be presenting. You may not recognize yourself.

Bottom Line:

The attitudes you present, sum you up - maybe unfairly or not. Be conscious. Be careful.

Nothing will get you just dismissed so quickly, as another person perceiving a bad attitude in yourself.

Attitudes are what people look for, when they do not know you. It is how most people operate in the impersonal world.

Making yourself correctly and honestly known, begins with you checking your attitudes before you meet. This is everybody's burden in our impersonal world.

Chapter 29

Why it Takes Ten Years to Get Over Being a Kid

Seriously, how can anyone say that it takes ten years to get over being a kid?

The answer to that question is take a hard look at what was happening when you were a kid, and what you are facing now as you leave a kid's personal world, and enter the impersonal world thereafter.

Your life, before reaching the age of 18, began when you were not much more than 18 inches long. This is when you first saw light, as a helpless infant. You were also totally clueless. Your life hung on the willingness of others to make your continued living possible.

The rigidity of this reality had you embracing your caregivers as if your life depended on their good will, which it did. From your standpoint, as a young kid, your relationship to your parents was not optional, and you knew it.

Come to age 18, you no longer need this life clinging relationship. But this is all you have ever known. You are now free to change it. But what is there to make you do it?

From your beginning to age 18, your life's activities happened as if your existence was jointly owned by yourself and your parents.

Getting over being a kid, is all about withdrawing your daily life's dependent relationship with your parent, and replacing it with ideas that are driven by your own free willed self-direction. It is a two step operation: withdraw and replace.

Withdrawing from your mindset of dependence cannot be done overnight, or in a year, or even in five years. It will take at least five years to take hold, and another five years to complete the job, as much as it ever will be completed. There is nothing hard and fast about how long all this will take. It varies with the individual.

But consider this:

As you grew older in your teens, you will remember how you began to do independent things without parent knowledge, and still the specter of their approval or not, never left your vision. Your existence was still a joint affair between you and your parents. This mindset is what has to change. It is the first move, if you are ever to get over being a kid.

The second move is to be also self conscious of how your life may be driven by acquiescence to peer pressure and conformity to what you see as a popular viewpoint of the media or the people now around you. You have to make yourself aware as to how your mind and desires are being influenced not just by your parents, but by your twin companions of media and peers that occupy the landscape of your mind. This is secondary to your parent problem.

After 18, when you are forced with gathering speed into an impersonal world, this joint existence with parents is less a practical possibility. Physical separation from your parents increases. And in the bright energy of your capable self care, it is less needed,

Nevertheless, that mindset will persist of your life being a joint affair between you and your primary caretakers, your parents. Because it is all you have ever known from your beginning.

But after 18, to create a replacing mindset of being self directed, and out from under a constant dependent approval of your parents, you will first have to accumulate the experience of separated thinking.

This means undergoing a reliving of the memories of all the occasions and details of the life you lived jointly with your parents, But doing so in your new setting of being physically apart and self-directed. The recurring seasons of the year have to pass, and holidays have to come and go, and you will have to live daily repetitions of sunrise to sunset.   But this time, the parade of life's events is under your own self-direction, edging out their association with your previous mindset of dependence.

You have to accumulate enough memories of living a life instigated by only your own direction, so that all expectation of dependence on parents has been replaced, and no longer lingers in the back of your mind.   Then you will find the newness of your independence no longer lingers as a struggling thought. It is just there. You are living as a self-directing person.

Withdrawing 18 years of dependence on your parents, your sole experience of life since birth, is a huge undertaking. It takes time to undergo. But does it really take 10 full years to get over this poise and posture of being a kid?   Yes, it normally will.   But there is more to consider to convince you.

Replacing the first 18 years of parent direction in your life, with a new power of self direction is a straight forward effort. It is a matter of having the bold curiosity and energy to ask the really basic questions about what in the world is really going on around you - surrounded as you are by zillions of people you don't know in an impersonal world. The question is:- How are you going to relate to it all?

This is a strange-to-you world you are entering, and in which you have had no serious experience.   So you try to stand back, and ask fundamental questions: About what all these people - whom you do not know - want; and personally, what they will want from you; where their heads are at; what they may expect from you; how to respond and deal with their expectations. Just like we explored these questions in previous chapters.

These are all focused questions, the meaning of which you need to pre-think. You need pre-thought answers to keep ready in your pocket, to enable a self direction for your life.

Because it is your standing on the answers to these rock bottom questions, that will enable you to keep in sight the self direction that you must have.

You need these answers to replace your withdrawal from an ingrained dependency on your parents and your peers and the media, and become your own person - which means a person self-directed.

This is why so many of these fundamental questions were asked, and explained in foregoing chapters. You will want to engage these discussions until you have settled answers for yourself in your own mind.

You just cannot go around life with a puzzled look. Only little kids get away with this. We all grow up - meaning we all have to chase our minds until we come to acknowledge what we must know.

Now all of this takes time. It will take a lot of thinking, reflecting, and absorbing. It is a complex task. But 10 years? To get over being a kid? How about 10,000 hours?

Consider this:

In 2007, Malcolm Gladwell explained in a book he called "Outliers", a strange but common sense appealing observation. It was startling in its directness. He said:

"The idea that excellence at performing a complex task requires a critical minimum level of practice surfaces again and again in studies of expertise. In fact, researchers have settled on what they believe is the magic number for true expertise: ten thousand hours."

"The emerging picture from such studies is that ten thousand hours of practice is required to achieve the level of mastery associated with being a world-class expert—in anything," writes the neurologist Daniel Levitin. "In study after study, of composers, basketball players, fiction writers, ice skaters, concert pianists, chess players, master criminals, and what have you, this number comes up again and again. Of course, this doesn't address why some people get more out of their practice sessions than others do. But no one has yet found a case in which true world-class expertise was accomplished in less time. It seems that it takes the brain this long to assimilate all that it needs to know to achieve true mastery. [Excerpts from: Gladwell, Malcolm, "Outliers." Little, Brown and Company, New York.]

Ten thousand hours of working and trying, to really be a master of any human performance. This is the human condition. This is what this observation is concluding; and Malcolm Gladwell provides further examples that credibly compel agreement.

So, are we saying here that it might take 10,000 hours to get over being a kid? The answer is 'yes', indeed it does makes sense that it would take 10,000 hours, and 10 years to do these hours.

Consider this: after age 18, whether you are going to school and studying, or you are on a regular work day job, you only have a limited number of hours available to you during the day where your mind has time for thinking as you chose. Discretionary mind time, let's call it.

Your mind time in a 24 hour day is largely confined and consumed by the must-do activity of sleeping, eating or washing, working or classes and studying. It would be fair to say - on average - that you only have in a normal day, some three hours for undriven thinking outside of these tasks - the only time available for thinking at your discretion. But even this is lessened now with the constant intrusion of media devices, cell phones, and your social emails and text messages.

This is about the extent of the daily time left for your mind to roam and reflect about yourself. It would probably be the only time you have to peruse your personal situation awareness. This is when you could observe and confirm your lessening reference to your parents in depending on their approval. This would be the time to form in its place your own self direction from your own reason and reflection.

If you agree that roughly three hours a day is all the time you would have in a regular day to yourself - your personal thoughts of where you are with your relationships and desires - then you are looking at a 1,000 hours a year. So you are indeed seeing that it does fully take ten years to put in the 10,000 hours that Gladwell points out is the human requirement to master any major development.

On this reflection then, this 10 years for getting over being a kid, is not an unnatural requirement for us humans - withdrawing from parental dependence, and replacing this dependence with your own self direction from your own considered ideas. There is a lot of construction to be done here: clearing the site, designing and building, and putting in the landscaping.

Is there any sense of urgency in all of this?

Well, there is just this: If you do not get over being a kid in ten years, it likely that you never will.

The reason would be that you never persisted with a self conscious effort to self-direct your life. The only method to really clear away your dependence on your parents to say who you are, is to firmly take yourself in hand and direct your life from your own sought out questions and resolved ideas.

Time spent on your own take-charge thinking on basic situational questions of your life, is the only path.

These basic situational questions of life that will drive your sense of self-direction have been discussed in the previous chapters - in broad and fundamental thinking. This is the path you must travel.

This is a mountain top trail, and mountain top thinking.

If you do not take this path, and walk to a height where you can look below and become aware of where you are, you will be a child lost in the forest beneath.

Sadly, you will simply become part of the milling crowd living with remnants of childhood dependence, waiting to be directed by whatever events happen to cross the wandering trail of a life that will befall you.

All of this takes time. As an infant, cutting your umbilical cord was a quick snip. As an 18-year-old, cutting your child dependency cord is not so simple. It was a tightly integrated mindset that you urgently needed in growing up. Down deep you know this now takes courage, to cut and face the unknown.

In the past, dependency fed you direction. This dependency has now got to be replaced with something else that will feed you direction. That's something else now has to come from you. That "you" means your ideas that truly come from what you honestly know and understand. This means change. The change is you.

Between 18 and 28 you are in the midst of change. You do have the energy, and at first you will have the willingness to change - to become self directed.

But beyond those initial 10 years you have after 18, such energy and willingness will diminish. You will probably be left at age 28 with whatever stage of becoming self directed, you will have then attained.

Of course, it is possible to evolve after age 28.

But a fundamental change in what we settle into being as humans, is not likely - after this age.

The edge is gone. There are no more graduations. The shock of life being so repetitious sets in. The force of boredom looms. It is the age when ambitions get trimmed for so many.

Those least equipped to deal with this, are those who failed to get over being a kid - failed to achieve self direction.

Chapter 30

The roads we all take - The paths underfoot

Do we know why?

There are down to earth underlying themes that run through our lives. They are seldom singled out for reflection. Like background music around us, that we never stop and think to give a name.

For instance, if at age 7 you were asked: "well, what are you doing now with your life?" You would probably think about the most important thing you were doing, and say you are going to school. And I would say, : "No, Tell me, what are you doing about your life?" You would say, "Well, I am growing up now."

And that is the background song that a kid wakes up to every morning - when he first sees light and movement. This is the solid earth underfoot that he will walk on this day. This is what his life is about, and he just knows it. Growing up is now the 'why' of his life - the what-to-do about his life.

But after this young person comes to his 18th year, he knows this is no longer true. So what now does he say to himself when getting up in the morning. What replaces 'growing up' as the 'why' of his life now?

It can no longer be about growing up. He has had his time for this. The what-to-do is now about something else. The music has changed. The ground underfoot is different. It will be hard for him to put a name to a new 'why' to his life. He probably has never heard this directly discussed. So he will have to be told.

What now has to be said to this new 18 year old boy, or 18 year old girl, is this: The 'why' of your life has now changed. You are walking the earth now with different ground under your feet. The what-to-do about your life is now different. You have finished the road of physically growing up.

The 'why' and what-to-do of your life is no longer to grow up, but to become. This is the time for you to become a person living a self directed life. You are putting away, and disassembling the dependent structure that surrounded you and protected you during you your time of physically growing.

This means shutting down the dependent directed energy that was the pushing engine of your growing up. This means changing out that engine to a new one that powers on different fuel. This fuel is a new energy and effort to create your own self direction.

You have ten years to operate this new engine to power your becoming this new self directed person.

If by misfortune you did not have much of a parent directed growing up, then it is time regardless of a difficult and uneasy past, to take yourself in tow and steady your life with the single goal of everyone your age: - to change from past dependencies to a new self directed life. It should be the fresh new song, the new 'why' of your life for the next ten years.

Just as at age 18 you are physically grown as much as you can ever be, at age 28 you will have changed to as much of a self directed person, as you are ever likely to be.

This becoming self directing is the 'why' of your life in the years from 18 to 28, just as growing up was the underlying 'why' of your life from 1 to 18 years.

But what happens at the end of these ten years? You will be about 28 years old. Your becoming years will be over. Then the underlying and driving music of the 'why' of your life will gradually turn to reside in a perspective that will occupy the rest of your life.

Then, when asked what your life is all about, the answer will be different, and be without a timeline, but like the other two periods in your life, it will still have a focus of something that has to be done. This time it is something that has to be asked and answered. It will be about 'why' of your life itself.

Your growing-up years are from birth to age 18. Your becoming years are from 18 to 28. From age 28 onwards, the self you have become, will be in what you will know as your 'seeking years' for the 'why of your own life - a task for the rest of your life time.

There is a connection in this sequence. The person that can go to the question of the 'why' of his life and seek answers, has to be, and can only be, someone who is in charge of his own mind and will. A question this serious, cannot be addressed by a weather vane mind - dependent on the direction of an outside force. It has to be directed by an inner force of a free will that chooses to focus one's entire being with all its awareness to seek an understanding.

This is why becoming a person of self directed powers is essential to understanding the life that has come to you.

Being self-directed will lead you to ask this question of 'why', with the gathered force of the whole of your being, and how to focus with discernment on answers.

Only a person who has achieved self direction can do this. This is why those ten becoming years after 18 are so important - after you have grown up sufficiently to take on with youthful energy this huge task of becoming self-directed as a human person.

Ultimately, you will understand this: if you are alive, and not asking 'why', you are just an animal.

A human person is born to ask this question. We know this, because we can ask this question. Animals cannot. The difference tells us what we are.

The rewards of being able to ask 'why', lie not in just the answers to which it leads us, but in the windows it opens for us along the way. The landscape we are able to see on this path of seeking answers provides reassurance and increasing contentment with the life we hold.

You know you are on this path, if every five years you can look back, and sense that you are simply happier as a person than you were five years ago. It is the reward of coming to know with a more contented certainty what you first began to vaguely understand.

When we question the 'why' of life, it is important to be critically aware of what we are doing in asking this question. It is no casual affair.

Asking such a question is not simple. It takes some thought and self reflection.

You have to watch yourself asking these questions to make sure you are asking as an honest being with an open mind, and that you are not searching in the shadows of your own predetermined answer.

For instance, it is not really an honestly truth-seeking question, if you ask if God exists, when you are thinking it could only be true if you are given material touchable evidence showing it to be true. You have a precondition. You are rejecting the possibility that there is another world of reality besides the one perceived by your five senses. So your question would not be an honestly wondering question as to whether God exists.

So you ought to be conscious of what's going on in your mind at different levels, when you do ask questions and seek the answers to the 'why' of your life. You cannot put pre-limits on your answers. You have to ask without preconditions.

This takes the kind of self-direction that you must capture in your becoming years. The 'you' that is asking, has to be a 'you' that is able to self direct the free-willed force of your whole being, to this seeking without preconditions for how your answer may turn out. You have to be a fearless full force human being.

The 'Why' of life is the question that everyone confronts, as the lengthening shadows of time touch the hard horizon of our physical limit.

But when you start to seriously seek this answer, and ask the question of 'why', you may just hear the echo of your own voice. Like being in a valley, you may just hear the rude repetition of your lonely voice echoing off the senseless rocks above. But that echo will be silenced if you persist in persisting, and move along and up, and keep asking as you climb every year.

You will come to understand - going from vague believing to really knowing - if you persist in honestly seeking.

It will no longer be just a matter of faith to believe. You will know.

Does this really happen? The answer is unexpected. It is even surprising.

It seems there is no person known, who has ever with the honest and directed force of his being, persisted with the question of 'why' about his or her human life, that has not come to a growing answer that brings understanding.

Can this be true? You will find out. You will discover.

It seems that the world's greatest secret is just lying out in the open - and it is this:

If you honestly and willfully ask, you <u>will</u> indeed come to understand answers to your question of the 'why' of your life.

Again, the secret is to honestly and with deliberate self direction, seek this answer with no lurking pre-determinations. Setting pre-limits is like your thinking that the reality of truth can only be disclosed by your five senses, or your insistence that you will not allow yourself to consider that you may owe your being to a higher power than your own existence.

You will not find a person who has come to disappointment in this quest - honestly seeking with a self direction free of conditions. None.

This has been boldly stated and deftly described in the literature of the world's oldest writings coming down to us from ancient times. In the Christian New Testament: "Ask and you shall receive" - "Knock and it shall be opened to you" is the most well known rendition of Christ. In fewer words: just knock.

And about five hundred years before, Buddha's teaching perceived this would be the only path: that ultimate reality and its truth cannot be taught to a human person. It can only be achieved by a person's own seeking, and seeking at the urging of his own free and self directed will.

But much of humanity remains just standing by the door.

So - the concerned hope for you is direct:

Try knocking. Seek. Persist.

Without seeking, nothing will happen.

You will not fail. None have failed before you

In Epilogue

To all my readers, now like past students slipping out of view as the hours together end, this has to be said:

It is always hard to let go of a class - a getting together.   It was always a wistful moment.

There were so many bright spirits of life that called out to be lingered with.

All I could say then, and now, looking forward with hope - :

Hey - Life is a river - see you downstream.

An Author's Note

You do not really need to know about the author. You need to know whether this book is worth your time to read, and will be of use to you. So it might be helpful to know why it was written.

Over a span of 50 years, I taught young people between the ages of 18 to 28 in various settings: college, university graduate programs, and business MBA courses for a Master's degree in Business Administration. This was not 50 years of teaching, but the years at the beginning and end of the period 1958 to 2007. During this time it was striking to see the changes in students' attitude toward learning. But what really caught my notice was how these young folks had so many of the same concerns and angst in their lives, though they were generations apart.

These were personal concerns about themselves. In after class discussions, they would broach questions that would normally go to a parent when they were younger, but not now when they are in ages over 18.

In the natural striving for independence, they turn to look for answers elsewhere. In the world they are now living after reaching the age of 18, there are no accepted places for just personal wondering, except sometimes the occasional Professor who will take the time to show a ready interest.

Everywhere in their 18 to 28 world - academic or not - they are surrounded with advice, but it is all about career building. There is little, mostly nothing, they could read about the state of life they are now going through, leaving a parent's intimate control, and heading into a never before experienced impersonal world. And the 'why' of all of this.

So in coming to an end of teaching with these thoughts in mind, I turned to writing The Becoming Years.

Now about the author who holds a Bachelor Degree from the Jesuit University of Detroit, a Master Degree in Political Philosophy from Duke University, and a Juris Doctor Degree from the University of Chicago Law School (a law degree).

All this education effort was interrupted by a pushing back from it going on too long. I took off for Europe, and ended up solo hitch-hiking for seven months from Cairo to Capetown, South Africa and onwards to Dakar, occupied with working at a Bank in Addis

Author's Note

Abba, Ethiopia, climbing Mt. Kilimanjaro, tracking gorillas in the Mountains of the Moon on the border of Uganda and Congo, enduring days stuck in hot Zanzibar living with a young monkey not house trained, not to mention the long nights marooned on ant hills while hitching rides along the roads of Northern Rhodesia, and dumping food off the back of a DC-3 aircraft over Cameroon while working for Dr. Albert Schweitzer in Lambarene, Gabon. Distraction over, I returned to school - reluctantly at first.

But before college degrees, there was four years of learning Latin and ancient Attic Greek, language and literature, in training with the Jesuits which included two (2) thirty day periods of absolute silence (no talking). This forced a solid look at the gift of life, and gave a further gift of calmness in living out whatever could happen.

During law school to support myself, I began teaching political science in an undergraduate college in a University, and International Law in its Graduate program. Teaching continued after law school until a few years later when I was appointed to the Legal Counsel Office of the United States Senate, Committee on Labor and Public Welfare.

Author'sNote

After several years in this position, I joined a Washington, DC law firm of Charles S. Rhyne, former President of the American Bar Association, and was focused on the firm's work before the Supreme Court of the United States.

In 1965, I became the first independent Counsel for the American Samoa Legislature, and was later appointed the first Federal Prosecutor in the Territory (to prosecute the Washington appointed outside Governor for trying to persuade the islanders not to elect their own Governor).

Some years later, I left the firm to become a resident lawyer in the U.S. Territory of American Samoa. Unlike Washington, D.C., a lawyer was needed in this community. There were none. I was their first resident U.S. Lawyer. I was their only lawyer then, and for a number of years. At last, a country lawyer with everyone to care for.

Years later, came a forced retirement due to a paralyzing accident in surfing with my ten year old son, David, whose pluck saved my life. After a time, but now in a wheelchair, I was able to go back to teaching in an MBA program in South Florida and Jamaica.

Author's Note

With my years of teaching in the classroom now ended, I wrote The Becoming Years with the thought, now a hope, that students I was never destined to meet, would read and engage their lives with a keener focus on the whole of what should be happening to them, and what they should be striving for, between the ages of 18 and 28 - and why.

There is no better moment for offering a caring suggestion to another human being, than in their Becoming Years 18 to 28.

And the reason is that the basic ideas first realized on beginning adulthood, are the trees that proudly line the road for the rest of life.

Thus - "It is easier to build strong youths, than to repair broken men," as Frederick Douglass wrote in 1895.

- G. A. Wray